P!NK

Raise Your Glass

P!NK

Raise Your Glass

ANNIE ZALESKI

PALAZZO

PALAZZO

This edition first published in 2023 by

Palazzo Editions Ltd
15 Church Road
London, SW13 9HE
www.palazzoeditions.com

A CIP catalogue record for this book is available from the British Library.

ISBN 978-1786751263
Bound and printed in China
10 9 8 7 6 5 4 3 2 1

Editor: Jo Rippon
Designed by Adelle Mahoney for Palazzo Editions

To my parents and my husband,
Matt – who always encourage
me to be strong

Previous: Pink performs at the Brit Awards, London, February 20, 2019

CONTENTS

INTRODUCTION

The era between the late nineties through Y2K and beyond was a golden age for pop music. For example, the *Billboard* Hot 100 U.S. singles chart for the week of March 4, 2000, featured an embarrassment of sonic riches. The Top Ten alone boasted a brisk punk hit from blink-182, swooning country ballads from Faith Hill and Lonestar, and singalong gems from teen-pop bands *NSync and Backstreet Boys.

However, the Hot Shot Debut of the week—meaning it was the highest-charting new song, at No. 25—went to the bouncy R&B kiss-off "There You Go," the first single released by Alecia Beth Moore, the artist better known as Pink—or P!nk. Co-written with two of the songwriters responsible for TLC's "No Scrubs," the song is a no-nonsense goodbye to a deadbeat ex. Although the guy tries to slink back into Pink's good graces, the singer isn't having any of his groveling or pleading; instead, she calls out his lies, straight-out says he's pathetic and sends him away.

"There You Go" eventually peaked at No. 7 in the US in April 2000, and also reached the Top Ten in the UK, Canada, Australia, and New Zealand. The success was no fluke: Pink immediately followed this up with an even bigger hit, "Most Girls," and, by the end of 2001, had also landed a No. 1 single as part of an ensemble covering Labelle's "Lady Marmalade." By then, Pink had made it clear: There was a new kind of pop star in town—one who was ferocious, fearless, and ready to shake up conventions.

Pink started honing this tenacity—and individuality—at a very young age. Born in 1979, she competed in gymnastics for years as a child before she was booted from the team for being too strong-willed. ("I was told, 'It's not an individual sport,'" she once divulged to *Women's Health*.) This toughness also came in handy in her personal life, as her parents divorced before her teenage years. Luckily, Pink was also already dabbling in music, both as a fan and as a performer, and this provided some solace from her turbulent home life. As a teenager, she started performing in Philadelphia clubs and by sixteen had landed a record deal as part of an R&B trio called Choice.

Opposite: Alecia Beth Moore, otherwise known as Pink, May 27, 2000

Right: Pink performs "Just Give Me A Reason" with Nate Ruess, at the 56th annual Grammy Awards in Los Angeles, California, January 26, 2014

"I am an R&B singer. I also am a gospel singer. I'm a punk-rock singer. And a pop singer. And a soul singer. All of that is me."

Opposite: Sporting a close-cropped shock of fluorescent (appropriately) pink hair, September, 2000

Despite being signed (and supported) by LaFace Records co-founder L.A. Reid, that group fizzled out by the late nineties. However, Pink more than rebounded with the success of her 2000 debut, setting the stage for a career that has taken many twists and turns. It's a cliché to say that a musician can do or perform anything, but in Pink's case it's true. Her voice is malleable—at various times she's unleashed a raspy growl, a liquid R&B croon, a punkish roar, and the speak-sing delivery of a smooth, slam poet—making her equal parts pop balladeer and rebellious rock star.

"I am an R&B singer," she said in 2019. "I also am a gospel singer. I'm a punk-rock singer. And a pop singer. And a soul singer. All of that is me."

Unsurprisingly, Pink dislikes being pigeonholed. That restlessness has prompted her to take multiple rewarding (and sometimes surprising) sonic detours. She sought out 4 Non Blondes' Linda Perry as a songwriting collaborator on 2001's *M!ssundaztood*, leading to a fresh-sounding album that redrew and expanded musical boundaries. Just two years later came *Try This*, a raucous rock-oriented album featuring collaborations with Rancid's Tim Armstrong and the electronic artist Peaches. In 2012, Pink and fun.'s Nate Ruess had a gigantic hit with a somber mid-tempo meditation, "Just Give Me One Reason." A few years later, she teamed up with Dallas Green from the Canadian indie-folk band City and Colour in the folk-inspired project You+Me. You're never quite sure where Pink is going to turn up next—or with whom she might be working.

That fluidity was by design, she told *Variety* in 2019. "I didn't want to be stuck in a box because there's nowhere to go. Also, if you want to blur lines, make people uncomfortable and question what they believe in just by looking at you, then you've got to take risks—you've got to be bold and go all out."

That description certainly fits her unpredictable (and even jaw-dropping) live shows. In a nod to her days as a gymnast, she's been known to perform a routine on a trapeze onstage, including for a memorable take on "Sober" at the 2009 MTV Video Music Awards. Separately, she's also incorporated aerial silks and acrobatics into her shows. These graceful and intricate flourishes have enhanced the power of her music and helped her become a massive live draw. In fact, her 2009–10 *Funhouse* global tour sold a staggering three million tickets.

Fittingly, Pink's fashions and appearance have also evolved with each new era. Early on, she sported a close-cropped shock of fluorescent (appropriately) pink hair, a look that she memorably once paired with a belly-baring Joan Jett T-shirt. You would have expected her to be at a Warped Tour rather than on *Total Request Live (TRL)*. (She's also sported a gigantic pink mohawk and a spiky black 'do'.) That freedom to mix and match styles and approaches remains strong. On one red carpet she might wear a smartly tailored three-piece suit; other occasions might feature a fancy dress that looks fit for a princess, a leather jacket over a dress, or something more outrageous, like a pair of pants with one leg. Pink embraces and celebrates androgynous looks and fashion, and has always made it clear she defines femininity on her own terms.

In interviews, Pink is also a refreshing presence: candid, honest, and never afraid to be reflective about her own shortcomings and strengths. That

Left: Pink shows off her trapeze skills at the MTV Video Music Awards in New York, September 13, 2009

Right: A beaming Pink with her Icon Award at the 2021 *Billboard* Music Awards, Los Angeles, California

introspection and vulnerability also permeates her song lyrics. She's never shied away from touching on politics, family trauma, sobriety, and dysfunctional relationships—not always the topics you expect to find in radio-friendly pop songs. Pink has also been quite open about living with depression and anxiety, and has praised the benefits of seeing a counselor. Her willingness to draw on such painful topics, and to speak frankly about what she deals with in her personal life, has turned her into a strong role model and mental health icon.

By now, Pink has more than proved that being an iconoclast has paid off critically and commercially. She's won shelves and shelves of awards—including three Grammys, a Daytime Emmy Award and seven MTV Video Music Awards, including the prestigious Video Vanguard Award—and in 2009 was named *Billboard*'s Pop Songs Artist of the Decade. She also won *Billboard*'s Woman of the Year award in 2013. And that's just scratching the surface.

More than two decades after the release of her debut single, Pink is no longer misunderstood—she enjoys the kind of creative freedom and stardom few others enjoy. It's all testament to her grit and self-confidence, as well as a willingness to live her truth, even if it goes against the grain. So, raise your glass to Pink—a dazzling performer, aspirational musician and pop icon.

billboard
MUSIC AWARDS
2021 Billboard Music Awards
ICON Award
PINK

TURNING PINK

You might point to Thanksgiving morning 1995 as the day Pink's life changed. It was 6.30am, and the then-sixteen-year-old was coming down after a long night spent reveling at a rave at a hip underground venue in Philadelphia called Club Fever. As Pink recalled to *Blender* back in 2002, things were winding down at the club when a friend suggested she hop onstage and commandeer the microphone.

"I'll do it," Pink recalls she responded, "if you can help me stand up." The impromptu performance didn't get her in trouble; in fact, a DJ told her to come back later that day to perform at the club's open mic night.

The invite had musical and social cachet: Back in 1995, Club Fever was a "hip-hop hotbed," according to the *Philadelphia Inquirer*. In fact, that year alone, the club hosted shows by rappers such as Notorious B.I.G., Naughty By Nature and Ol' Dirty Bastard, in addition to giving local talent a shot. At open mic night, Pink rallied and sang Mary J. Blige—and did well enough to earn a weekly performance slot. The tough-talking, rowdy teenager had taken her first steps to fulfill a long-held dream: becoming a professional musician.

"I knew at 2 or 3 that I'd be a singer," she told *USA Today* in 2012. "I believe that you sign up for this life before you get here. I thought if I couldn't get on *Star Search* by the time I was 9, my life was over. I never pictured anything else."

Previous: Pink arrives at the 2nd annual Teen Choice Awards, August 6, 2000, Santa Monica Air Center, California

Above left: Onstage at Madison Square Garden opening for *NSYNC on their *No Strings Attached* tour, July 25, 2000

Above: Pink and her mom, Judith, arriving at the 44th Grammy Awards, in Los Angeles, California, 2002

> "I knew at 2 or 3 that I'd be a singer. I believe that you sign up for this life before you get here. I thought if I couldn't get on *Star Search* by the time I was 9, my life was over. I never pictured anything else."

Pink's early life didn't hint at future superstardom. Born on September 8, 1979, in Doylestown, Pennsylvania, a small borough located twenty-five miles north of Philadelphia, she was the second child of Judy, who worked as a nurse, and Jim Moore, a Vietnam veteran and former boxer who sold insurance. (Her older brother, Jason, eventually followed in their dad's footsteps and embarked on a long, distinguished military career.) Early on, health issues were Pink's biggest concern. She was born with a collapsed lung and was diagnosed with asthma at age two; she started taking soccer, gymnastics and dance lessons at an early age to stay active.

Her family wasn't overly into music—except for her dad, who passed down his rebellious (and musical) side to his daughter. "I had hair down to my shoulders, drove a motorcycle, played in a band," he told the *Philadelphia Inquirer.* "My beard was so long, I had to wear a rubber band around it when I rode. I wasn't exactly an angel myself." Pink and her dad shared a deep love for pianist-rocker Billy Joel; in fact, the first concert she saw was Joel's, when she was just two years old. "You were like a god that I prayed to as a child," she told Joel during a 2014 radio special. "My dad was my other god. And I got to see my dad become happy when your songs came on, and we sang them together. It's shaped and painted my whole life."

Joel wasn't the only musician she admired. Growing up in the 1980s, Pink also embraced the vibrant pop and rock music of the decade. She loved teen pop star Debbie Gibson and the boy band New Kids on the Block (NKOTB); somewhat sheepishly, she once admitted to seeing the fresh-faced group live. "I'm not going to lie—I did," she told *The Face*, noting that NKOTB's bad boy, Donnie Wahlberg, was her favorite. "And I screamed."

She had a poster of big-haired rocker Jon Bon Jovi on her wall, and was utterly devastated when he got married to his high-school sweetheart in 1989.

Opposite: Pink and her dad, Jim, at the 2000 *Billboard* Music Awards, in Las Vegas

MUSIC AWARDS
FOX
MGM GRAND
FOX
MGM GRAND

"I did not come out of my room for a week," she told Bon Jovi himself years later, while she accepted the Icon of the Year award from him at the 2021 *Billboard* Music Awards. "When I ripped your poster off the wall, I replaced you with [Skid Row's] Sebastian Bach. I'm very glad that you found lasting love, Jon, but you broke my heart!"

While it's typical for kids to have ever-changing musical tastes, Pink was an especially voracious listener; in one interview with *Variety*, she name-checked rappers 2 Live Crew, punks Green Day, and musicals such as *Les Misérables* and *Phantom of the Opera* as favorites. "Musically, I've never fit into anywhere. I just kind of like everything," she told Carson Daly, the former host of MTV's *Total Request Live* (*TRL*), in a 2019 TODAY interview on NBC. "My first cassette tape I bought was Mary J. Blige. My first vinyl was Mamas and the Papas, my first crush was Jon Bon Jovi and I sang opera. So I've always been in just a mystery bag."

But like many music fans, Pink also desired to be onstage, just like her idols. She sang gospel music in church and started taking vocal lessons at age nine. "When I was in elementary school, I told the teachers, 'Be nice to me, since I'm going to be big someday,'" Pink disclosed to her hometown newspaper, the *Doylestown Intelligencer*, in 2013. "They were, like, 'All right, sure, sure.'" But even then, Pink backed up her youthful swagger with action. An early video of her as a child singing Madonna's "Oh Father" at a recital revealed sophistication beyond her years. Even at that young age, Pink had a gift for capturing deep, genuine emotion.

That sensitivity came from a very real place, as Pink's home life could be rough. "My household was World War III," she said in a 2009 episode of VH1's *Behind the Music*. "My parents hated each other. I knew what divorce was—and what it meant—before I really knew what marriage meant." In interviews, she described a stressful environment with lots of disagreements and yelling. "It was a very tip-toey environment, like walking on eggshells," she told *The Face*. "It was just so tense, all the time." She shares that she remembers

being three years old and "crying myself to sleep every night, praying to God to make it better. Like, how can I fix my family? Because kids always think it's their fault." Even still, when her parents finally decided to get divorced—when she was eight years old—it was a hard pill to swallow. "I just remember running upstairs into my mom and dad's bed," she said on VH1. "I was completely devastated. And I was just hysterical."

Pink had many outlets for her angst, anger and sadness. She spent eight years as a competitive gymnast, and was talented enough to reach elite events at the state levels. ("The vault used to kill me," she said in 2000.) Despite her skills, however, her ferocious ambition stymied her progress. "If I got second place I wasn't satisfied. I had to get first place or it wasn't gonna work for any of us. So they kicked me out for having a non-team-like attitude."

That competitive spirit also propelled Pink in the skateboarding world. In fact, she was a very serious skater who practiced her craft both at home and at skate camp in the Pocono Mountains. "I'd go to the parks and skate ramps," she told *Launch*. "Half-pipe was my thing—like, six-foot, four-foot. I was good." However, not everybody took her seriously—which only made her more determined to succeed. "The thing that drove me was when people told me I couldn't do something," she added. "I was climbing trees instead of playing with Barbies just because people said I couldn't do it. So with skating, for me, everybody called me a poseur, so I was going to get good at it."

In addition to these activities, Pink also became more serious about music. At thirteen, she was in a rock band called Middleground that appeared in clubs and talent shows. Being in a band staved off her boredom ("It kept me from being home and it was just something to do," she told *Launch*) but also provided one of her first

Pink grew up listening to piano-rocker Billy Joel (above, left), but also loved the vibrant pop sound of eighties teen stars such as Debbie Gibson (above, far left) and NKOTB (above, right, from L-R: Danny Wood, Donnie Wahlberg, Jordan Knight, Joe McIntyre, and Jon Knight.)

Opposite: Pink at the MTV Video Music Awards, 2000

songwriting outlets. "I always loved singing. But with the rock band, I got to write my own music too, because it was just us kids ... We won talent show after talent show after talent show." Video from that time showed her looking very early-nineties' chic, with an oversized plaid shirt, nose stud, and super-short hair, but wailing on grunge-inspired songs with the poise and power of a vocalist twice her age. In a VH1 documentary, her mom remembered being stunned by Pink's lyrics, which were also rather wise for her age. "Her initial writings were always very introspective. Some of it was very black, and very deep, almost worrisome."

She earned the nickname Pink during adolescence. The name's origin story varies. In one interview, she said friends called her this because her face flushed crimson when she got embarrassed. At other times, she said the moniker came from the character Mr. Pink from the Quentin Tarantino movie *Reservoir Dogs*. However, she told a *USA Today* interviewer that the latter interpretation is "the Disney version" of her origin story. "Others are R-rated." Going by an interview with *Playboy*, another source of her nickname had something to do with a friend of hers commenting on the color of her private parts.

That name change coincided with wild, raucous teenage years. She told a magazine interviewer in 2002 she had been smoking a pack of cigarettes a day since the age of nine, and *Playboy* that she started smoking weed at age eleven and subsequently started dabbling in other drugs at thirteen. Pink also started running away from home and was involved in illegal activities, including selling drugs such as ketamine. "I realized that I'd have a side project if I turned my mom's house into a K-house when she was at work," she told VH1. "So I would cook it and sell it—and people would be in K-holes all over my house."

Her crimes later expanded to include theft—Pink shoplifted "shopping bags and trash bags full of clothing from department stores," she told the *Honolulu Advertiser,* as well as a copy of the movie *Showgirls* from Blockbuster Video—and breaking and entering into the house of a girl who stole her diary. She didn't last long in jobs at fast food places such as Pizza Hut, Burger King, and McDonald's due to her bad behavior; in one interview, she talked about coming to work while still tripping on acid. "I was the perfect kid, I had fun when I was little, I climbed trees, total tomboy," she told *The Sun*, "but when I hit the double digits, it turned. I just went crazy."

Quite understandably, she earned a reputation for being the teen her peers were told to avoid. "Other people's parents wouldn't let me come over when I was a

"When I was in elementary school, I told the teachers, 'Be nice to me, since I'm going to be big someday.'"

"I was the perfect kid, I had fun when I was little, I climbed trees, total tomboy, but when I hit the double digits, it turned. I just went crazy."

kid," she told *The Guardian*. "I was the shithead. No one wanted their kid anywhere near me. I was the runaway, I was the fuck-up, I was the one that had the mouth, I was always in trouble." Naturally, her behavior also caused immense stress at home. She and her mom especially had a very strained relationship. "My mom tried to get me to talk to someone when I was fourteen to erase all the stuff she put on me," Pink told *Rolling Stone* in 2002. The therapy didn't take. "The therapist would ask me about my day, and I'd tell her that at lunch I had a vision of breaking a bottle over someone's head. After the fifth session, she told my mother there was nothing she could do."

Speaking to *Variety* in 2019, Pink shared that her teenage rebellion continued to be volatile. She dropped out of school, and her mom kicked her out of the house at age fifteen. "I felt grown at a very young age. They just couldn't stop me—and they knew they wouldn't be able to stop me—so they figured it would be better for our relationship if they supported me." This took the form of Pink moving in with her father, as their personalities meshed better. "I'm him reincarnated. I have his attitude, his mouth, his insight ... everything," she told a website called Lindzi.com. "Whenever we talk, it's like I'm talking to myself, but a much wiser version." Indeed, Pink's dad provided her needed guidance and structure. To *The Guardian*, she added: "He was an angry man, but the greatest life teacher; he gave me opinions to rebel about. My anger had a direction as he made me aware of politics, government, aware of being a survivor."

Outside of her dad, other adults saw Pink's potential—and luckily could tell she wasn't a bad seed. "I remember her out on the corner with the other 'hoodlums,'" Blair Elliot, the owner of the Doylestown independent record store, Siren Records, told the *Doylestown Intelligencer* in 2013, "and I use the term 'hoodlums' in a loving way. We loved those kids." They had "a lot of energy and ideas," Elliot added, especially Pink. "She was able to put all of that to good use. She willed herself to the incredible career she has today."

Indeed, despite all of her wild ways and delinquent behaviors, Pink knew she needed to clean up her act. In fact, she says the last day she ever did drugs was that Thanksgiving all-nighter. "I was an experimental kid; put it that way," she told *The Face*. "I was very curious and I'm glad I was curious at a young age, because I would never take that part of my life back. It made me very aware of what things can do, and how much fun and how much disaster you can have in your life at the same time. And it wasn't for me."

Putting that part of her life behind her ended up paying off quicker than she imagined. A few weeks after Pink started singing at Club Fever, she was spotted by a scout for MCA Records. Impressed with her talent, she was recruited to join an R&B girl group called Basic Instinct. Though just a teenager, Pink was on her way to a career in music.

Opposite: At the 1999 Teen Choice Awards, in Santa Monica

SINGER'S CHOICE

"When I first met her, she was sweet, charming, amazing, talented and gifted. She had a not-so-nice attitude and her eyes set firmly on the prize of being a star. Her talents are as much her voice as her attitude, though."

ANTONIO "L.A." REID

Girl groups have played an integral role in popular music history. In the 1940s, the close harmonies of The Andrews Sisters drove the conversation. The 1960s spawned pop luminaries The Ronettes, Martha & The Vandellas, and The Supremes, while the following decade saw the emergence of Labelle and The Pointer Sisters. Two decades later, the nineties ushered in another golden age for pop and R&B girl groups. Early in the decade, TLC, Jade, SWV and En Vogue permeated the charts, paving the way for Spice Girls, Atomic Kitten, and Wild Orchid. As the nineties ended, the next generation of groups that came along—3LW, Blaque, Destiny's Child, Dream, and B*Witched, to name a few—intersected with the trend for teen pop.

Pink thought she had found her golden ticket singing with a Philadelphia-based R&B girl group called Basic Instinct. However, her tenure was short-lived—according to Pink, she was bounced from the group for being white. She quickly tried out for another R&B act called Choice at (of all places) a McDonald's in Philadelphia. Eager to join the group, Pink gave the other musicians involved plenty of musical options, she told *The Face*. "I was like, 'I can sing Whitney, I can sing Mary, I can sing Green Day, I can sing Janis Joplin, I can sing Billy Joel, *Phantom of the Opera*. What genre are you looking for? I can do that!'"

She passed the local audition with flying colors. "We sang, and it instantly meshed," group member Sharon Flanagan told the *Press of Atlantic City* in 2006. "There were sparks."

Choice became a trio with Pink, Flanagan, and New Jersey native Chrissy Conway. They sent out a demo tape to various labels, sparking a bidding war that culminated in a trip to Atlanta to audition for LaFace Records. Co-founded by Antonio "L.A." Reid and Kenneth "Babyface" Edmonds, the label was a nineties' powerhouse, home to superstars such as TLC, Toni Braxton and Outkast.

Reid was impressed by Choice and ended up signing the group in summer 1996, when Pink was still just sixteen years old. It was clear to him the teen was

Previous: Pink performs onstage at Webster Hall in New York City, October 25, 2000

Opposite: Kenneth 'Babyface' Edmonds and L.A. Reid pictured together in 2017

Junior Mints

Left: The US poster for the 1996 Shaquille O'Neal movie, *Kazaam*. Pink, as part of girl group Choice, featured on the movie's soundtrack.

Opposite: Pink's former Choice bandmate, Chrissy Conway went on to form Christian girl group, ZOEgirl, pictured here in 2003

a future star. "When I first met her, she was sweet, charming, amazing, talented and gifted," Reid told *The Guardian*. "I couldn't take my eyes off her. She's pretty in a tough way; she's not just a cutesy little thing. She had a not-so-nice attitude and her eyes set firmly on the prize of being a star. Her talents are as much her voice as her attitude, though."

For the next two years, Choice worked hard at building a career. The trio moved to Atlanta, taking advantage of LaFace-provided vocal and physical training, as well as housing. They cut demos, with the goal of finishing an album, but generally kept a low profile. Their first officially released studio song was on the soundtrack of the Shaquille O'Neal 1996 film *Kazaam*. Introducing younger acts via soundtracks was a common major label strategy in the 1990s, and Choice was in good company. Their harmony-heavy slow R&B song called "Key to My Heart" appeared alongside Usher, Backstreet Boys, Boyz II Men's Nathan Morris, Spinderella, and music from O'Neal himself.

Other Choice songs eventually surfaced, either in full or in part, that were much in the same vein as "Key to My Heart": polished R&B songs that showed off the trio's lovely voices. Years later, Flanagan expressed some doubts about the releases. "There were songs we liked that didn't make it," she told the *Press of Atlantic City*. "This was our first album, but I wasn't really proud ... I remember thinking, I kind of want this to end; I don't want to fake the funk. I knew there was something missing for me." Pink was also apparently skeptical, going by what she told *Rolling Stone* in 2002: "We were singing these pop songs that were, I don't know, *unseasoned*."

Still, Pink enjoyed her time in the group, she later recalled in a 2004 Yahoo! interview. "I love harmony, I love harmonizing, there's nothing like it. When you are with two girls and you all live together and sing together and breathe together and cry together, the sound that you three can make together, it's beautiful. We used to sing gospel songs and rock and every kind of song, and it was just beautiful." Flanagan too had fond memories of being with the other girls, recalling tons of laughter ("We could turn an airplane ride into our own comedy show") and their unique chemistry. "I remember the three of us being deeply moved by our voices together. It was something very special."

After several years of hard work, Choice did finish an album. However, the powers-that-be declined to release it, which effectively killed the group's momentum and put their career in jeopardy. (Complete albums being shelved or cancelled before they can be released happens more than you might think, especially if the album is by a newer act.) The label still thought Pink had promise as a vocalist, however—albeit under certain conditions. As Pink recalled in a revealing 2019 *Variety* interview, after Choice's album release was cancelled, she was asked to make an impossible decision.

Either stay in the group and be stuck in limbo, or step out on her own as a solo artist and have a second chance at musical success.

"I had to be the one to decide to go solo and not L.A. Reid, my record company president, because that would be him interfering in a [pre-existing] contract," she explained. "He told me behind the scenes: 'If you don't go solo, I'm never going to support you — however, it has to be your idea.' So that was the first tricky part."

Through a modern lens, it's staggering to think that Pink—who was barely out of adolescence—had the burden of making such a huge choice by herself. Thankfully, she was mature enough to understand what a big responsibility this was and didn't make the decision lightly. She weighed her options carefully, taking into consideration the loyalty she felt to her friends and bandmates; their shared history together; and the hard work they collectively put into making Choice a success. "[It] was horrifying and I felt like I was a huge piece of shit," she said about trying to come to a decision. "I threw up for a week thinking about these girls and what we had been through together and how unfair that was to them and just how absurd it all was."

Pink also turned to Reid to help her figure out the best direction to take. "I remember talking about it on the phone and he said, 'Babe, when you pictured yourself as a little girl up on stage, did you picture yourself in a group or did you picture yourself ramming your f—ing stubborn-ass head through the world by yourself?' And I was like: 'That.' And he was like: 'Then, don't waste the rest of your life because of guilt.'"

In hindsight, even if Pink didn't end up going solo at that point, chances are she would've gone off on her own eventually, thanks to her strong-willed personality. "With a group, you have to compromise yourself," she told Yahoo! "The three of us were from different walks of life, basically, and I'm so passionate about what I do, so hands-on, it's hard for me to be able to agree with two other people—let alone women, you know what I mean? Being in a group is hard, but it was cool in my situation because we all wanted to do different things."

Indeed, after Choice dissolved, the three members scattered. Conway found musical success of

“I really wanted this Bebe catsuit but it was like $300, and I told L.A. [Reid], ‘I’ll re-sign but I want that catsuit.’”

her own with the Christian teen pop group ZOEgirl. Signed to Sparrow Records, the trio won a Dove Award (the Christian equivalent of the Grammy Award) for New Artist of the Year in 2002 and had a No. 1 single on Christian radio with the single “All of My Heart.” Conway remembered her time in Choice—and Pink—fondly. “We had a great time,” she told Pennsylvania newspaper the *Morning Call* in 2005. “We were doing what we loved and she was a crazy girl. Of course we had plenty of excitement all the time with her—there was never a dull moment.” Flanagan also stayed in music, performing jazz, blues and R&B songs in local New Jersey venues and even writing her own songs.

After Pink decided to go solo, the pieces of the puzzle took a while to fall into place. Business considerations trumped musical ones—and Pink’s support system fell apart. As she told *Variety*. “So I no longer have a record contract, I no longer have managers, and since they were paying for us to live [in Atlanta], I no longer had a place to live. ...What do I do?” Decades later, Pink also revealed she had a miscarriage at age seventeen, squarely during the time she was in Choice, which no doubt was also an emotional experience. “I was going to have that child,” she told *USA Today* in 2019. “But when that happens to a woman or a young girl, you feel like your body hates you and like your body is broken, and it’s not doing what it’s supposed to do.”

Post-Choice, Pink’s solution was to skip town and move to New York City, where she had connections, and figured she could write songs and work out her next steps. Luckily, she was also hired to sing backup on albums by Diana Ross, Kenny Lattimore and 98 Degrees, which kept her afloat financially. Pink also met a publishing executive who took a liking to her songwriting and offered her a deal. “This publisher walked in and said, ‘What would it take to get you to sign a publishing deal?’” she told *Variety*. “I’m broke at this point —I have like $20. And I go, ‘One million dollars!’ I was joking. And he goes, ‘OK, I’ll see you on Monday.’ I was like, ‘Huh? Shit, I should have said two!’”

Unfortunately, the missing-in-action management team behind Choice also came back into her life, just in time to reap the benefits of her windfall. “They go, ‘You never fired us. By the way, little girl, when you want to fire people, you have to put it in writing. So we’re taking this advance.’ And they took all my money.” Her naivete also came into play as she renegotiated her record deal with LaFace Records. The label’s offices were across the street from a mall Pink frequented, and the glitzy stores offered tantalizing options for the young artist. “I really wanted this Bebe catsuit [there] but it was like $300,” she told *Variety*. “And I told L.A. [Reid], ‘I’ll re-sign but I want that catsuit.’ So that’s what I re-signed for, basically. I didn’t do a great job but I didn’t care—I just wanted to put a record out.”

Despite the ups and downs she had already experienced along the way, Pink signed her solo deal with LaFace Records and was excited for what the future would bring. Although the coming years would bring more victories *and* challenges, she recalled nothing but good memories of those very early days in a 2019 TODAY interview. “I slid in at the end of actual record deals and artist development and time to find yourself at a real record company that felt like a family, that would rise and fall with you. It was cool. It was a good time to start.”

Opposite: Pink, circa 2000

THERE YOU GO

Previous: Pink onstage, 2000

Opposite: Arriving for the 6th annual Soul Train Lady of Soul Awards, September 2, 2000, in Santa Monica, California

Many musicians take a while to find their unique voice and niche. That's why so many now-famous artists release debut albums that sound so different from their most recognizable work. Take Radiohead's first album, *Pablo Honey*, a grungy, shoegazing record that sounds nothing like the band's later electronic experiments. Or Alanis Morissette, whose first few albums released in Canada were full of glossy Top Forty pop songs—a far cry from her later music, which featured deeply confessional lyrics and drew on influences from rock and folk.

Pink's debut album, *Can't Take Me Home*, is also an outlier in her catalog. That was obvious from the generic cover image, which depicts her looking like a robot behind mirrored sunglasses and a lacquered pink buzzcut. With songs co-written by R&B heavyweights such as Babyface and Kandi Burruss, the full-length release boasts well-crafted music that fit perfectly with the Y2K era's beat-heavy, pop/hip-hop hybrids. "Let Me Let You Know" is a meditative ballad; "Hell Wit Ya" is rock-kissed rap; and "Private Show" is a sizzling R&B jam. The longing, piano-driven "Love Is Such a Crazy Thing" was a holdover from her days in Choice; in fact, her former bandmates added backup harmonies on the song.

However, *Can't Take Me Home* distinguishes itself from other debuts because Pink herself co-wrote multiple songs. "I think writing is a requirement for artists," she told MTV News prior to the release of *Can't Take Me Home*. "Now, so many artists are so polished, and a lot of them don't write. But I have an awful lot of issues, and I'm just glad they gave me the chance to prove myself. I'm not an artist that gets up and sings love songs. I'm not in love. It's not going on in my life, so I can't be passionate about it."

Indeed, *Can't Take Me Home* is honest about rocky relationships and contains its fair share of breakup songs—likely in no small part because Pink and her long-term boyfriend from Philadelphia had split while she was making the album. She caught him cheating with not one, but two other women. "It was the most painful, weirdest, most unhealthy relationship ever," she told *The Face*. "I thought I was in love, but I was

"I think writing is a requirement for artists. Now, so many artists are so polished, and a lot of them don't write. But I have an awful lot of issues, and I'm just glad they gave me the chance to prove myself."

MTV
MUSIC TELEVISION

just kind of dependent." No wonder she brought such sarcastic sass to "There You Go," and its depictions of a lame ex-boyfriend.

Can't Take Me Home's themes are rather sophisticated for a debut album. For example, Pink wrote the brisk, electro-kissed title track about a rocky relationship. "I was with someone of a different race, and he didn't want to take me home to his mother because he didn't think that his mother would approve of me, basically," she revealed in an interview. "Split Personality," meanwhile, is about her own tumultuous inner life—and how she feels like she's "two girls trying to blend, trying to vibe," as she puts it in the lyrics. On a similar note, the slow jam "Stop Falling" contains lyrics that foreshadow Pink's later forays into self-empowerment. In no uncertain terms, the song flips the bird to stereotypical behavior—for example, the idea that being young means she needs to be protected, or that being a woman means she's in search of a partner. "I'm not looking for love," she explained in an interview. "I'm not looking for all the stress that it brings. I'm looking for better days, and either give me everything or nothing at all."

Pink released *Can't Take Me Home* on April 4, 2000, the same week her debut single, "There You Go," reached its chart peak on the *Billboard* Hot 100 singles chart. In the record's liner notes, she dedicated the album "to my daddy, my hero, my glue, my mentor. You have helped me more than most would help themselves." Elsewhere on the page, she also thanked her mom "for loving me

Opposite: Pink and music video director Dave Meyers celebrate at the MTV Video Music Awards, New York City, August 28, 2002

Above: R&B star, Kandi Burruss, who worked with Pink on her debut album, *Can't Take Me Home*

Opposite: Pink pictured with Carson Daly, the then host of MTV's *Total Request Live (TRL)*

even when it was hard." *Can't Take Me Home* debuted at a respectable No. 26 on the *Billboard* 200 albums chart in April, its peak position. Elsewhere in the world, the album did much better, with a No. 10 showing in Australia and a UK No. 13 peak.

As "There You Go" sped up the charts in late winter 2000, the music video also started making waves. The clip was directed by Dave Meyers, a celebrated director who would play a big part in Pink's visual presentation for years to come. The highly stylized clip matches the song's theme; Pink, in no uncertain terms, telling off her no-good ex. In the video, her ex is shown playing videogames, lying about having another girl in his place and then trying to bum a ride from Pink. In response, she sends her motorcycle flying in the air and right through his apartment window. Throughout, she gives major attitude to the camera while wearing a variety of trendy outfits, such as a yellow furry coat over a magenta crop top, or a lime-green turtleneck sweater.

"I think this is the prettiest I've ever looked, and will ever look," she told *Billboard* about the video. "I'd just started riding motorcycles. I almost crashed 85 times." This is no exaggeration, because she—incredibly—did most of her own stunts in the clip, including leaping off the motorcycle as it soared. Only a near-miss prevented her from doing the most death-defying moves, she later told *Newsday*, "After I crashed into a trailer and almost hit a UPS truck, they told me they were going to get a stunt person." It's difficult to imagine a record label today allowing promising young talent to risk their lives doing dangerous stunts—but it's also not hard to imagine Pink very stubbornly insisting that she could handle herself just fine.

Due to these colorful visuals, Pink and MTV developed a close relationship. She appeared on the channel's spring break in March, singing in front of partying college students on the beach. On April 17, the video for "There You Go" made its debut on the *TRL* countdown at No. 8, marking Pink's first appearance on the influential show. The clip stayed on the show one more day, resurfacing briefly in May after Pink herself appeared on the show. In an interview sandwiched between popular videos of the time—Kid Rock's "American Bad Ass," Christina Aguilera's "I Turn to You" and Bloodhound Gang's "The Bad Touch"— she and host Carson Daly bantered about her musical background, *Can't Take Me Home,* and her outfit. Pink wore a black-and-white jester hat, flared white pants that were folded down at the waist ("I don't believe in buttons," she quipped), a belly-baring black jacket, and rose-tinted sunglasses.

For three months in the first half of 2000, Pink opened for *NSYNC on the boy band's *No Strings Attached* tour. Not only was it a great career opportunity—she was able to perform at legendary arenas such as Madison Square Garden, as well as in packed stadiums—but touring itself was also a good experience. At one point, she even went on an ice cream date to the restaurant Friendly's with *NSYNC's Joey Fatone. "Such a sweetheart," she told *Glamour*. "He asked my dad's permission."

More doors opened for Pink. On September 2, she co-hosted the long-running *Soul Train* TV show's Lady of Soul Awards and, later that same week, had her video for "There You Go" in the running for Best New Artist at the MTV Video Music Awards. (Unfortunately, she lost to Macy Gray's "I Try.") Several months later, Pink earned what was then her highest charting single, as "Most Girls" reached its peak of No. 4 on the *Billboard* Hot 100 on November 25. The song was also

PAPD

Opposite and previous page: Pink in concert May 27, 2000, in New Orleans, Louisiana

a dancefloor favorite, and spent four weeks atop *Billboard*'s Hot Dance Music Maxi-Singles Sales chart.

The music video for "Most Girls", also directed by Dave Meyers, was a continuation of the empowerment vibe of "There You Go." (Literally: The video for the earlier song is playing on a TV at the start, as Pink is doing push-ups.) She deals with a car that's ransacked and destroyed, gets her anger out in a boxing ring (where she punches another woman) and finally links up with a man worth her time. In between these scenes are seriously impressive displays of choreographed moves led by Pink and a bevy of acrobatic, buff dancers.

All of this activity helped boost *Can't Take Me Home*'s sales, and the album was certified double-platinum by the end of the year.

Understandably, like what happens with many successful artists, Pink's ascent brought about a backlash. In an early 2001 interview with *NME*, Pink admitted experiencing "prejudice" for a range of things, including her gender, her shocking pink hair and her outspokenness. However, Pink also cited "being white" and being thought of as Black "as things for which she received criticism." These two things seem to be in conflict; however, elsewhere in the interview, Pink acknowledged receiving criticism because she was a white artist singing contemporary R&B. She brushed off this musical critique. "You get criticism for everything you do. The important thing is the respect I've gotten. Hosting the Lady of Soul Awards, being nominated for R&B and soul categories—it's a breakthrough thing."

For some people, Pink's problematic persona circa *Can't Take Me Home* went beyond her being a white woman becoming a star with soul and R&B. Years later, the feminist website Jezebel delved into Pink's music, videos and interviews to explore her racial line-blurring circa *Can't Take Me Home*. Her "aesthetic copied black trends," wrote author Ashley Reese, noting specifically Pink's "baggy pants and tank top combo" and close-cropped haircut. At this stage in her career, Pink also "played to the confusion over her race" in interviews, Reese added, which "suggest that she may have relished her racial ambiguity." For example, the article quoted an online chat during which Pink answered the

"There is no demographic for me. It's young, old, moms, daughters, every color of the rainbow, from every part of life. Everyone can relate to me. It's cool."

fan question, "Do you get offended when people mistake you for Black?" by replying: "Of course I don't get offended. We're all pink on the inside."

This phenomenon of racial ambiguity wasn't necessarily unique to Pink in this era. "Pink's responses to questions about her race suggest a kind of tension that pervaded both pop and politics at the time," continued Reese. "Pink's answers simultaneously claimed blackness—playing into the music industry's fetish of white artists presenting as black—while refusing to acknowledge the realities, as well as the very existence, of race." The article cited a 2001 *Baltimore Sun* interview in which Pink said, "I don't choose to get caught up in the whole color scene."

Speaking to *NME* around this time, Pink echoed this sentiment when describing what happens when she does an in-store appearance. "There is no demographic for me. It's young, old, moms, daughters, every color of the rainbow, from every part of life. Everyone can relate to me. It's cool." Certainly, this was a function of Pink's versatile voice and chameleonic talent; she was the rare pop star that *could* sing any style of music, and do it well.

In her piece, Jezebel's Reese concluded that there were no straightforward or clear-cut answers to questions of Pink's authenticity or whether she was guilty of cultural appropriation. She didn't let Pink off the hook fully, however: "While Pink's blasé interrogation with race was shallow, elementary, and eye-roll inducing, I'm almost inclined to put Pink's antics in the 'not that deep' category, if only because her reign as the token black-white girl of R&B was blessedly short."

That last part is certainly true. In a gesture that would soon come to be seen as characteristic, when the era of *Can't Take Me Home* ended, Pink slammed the door firmly on that chapter of her career—and moved on to something else without looking back.

Above left: Co-hosting the 6th annual Soul Train Lady of Soul Awards with actor Shemar Moore (left) and SisQó (right) in Santa Monica, California, 2000

Right: At the MTV Music Video Awards, 2000

Pink: Animal Rights and Social Issues

Pink has always stood up for underdogs and the unappreciated. Unsurprisingly, that means she's been a fierce advocate for animal rights since she was a kid. "Every book report I did in school was on cruelty to animals," she told MTV in 2006. "I write lots of angry letters for PETA [People for the Ethical Treatment of Animals]. I believe in everything they do."

Her advocacy first rose to public awareness after she filmed the video for 2001's "Just Like a Pill." The clip featured a scene where she sang in front of an elephant. Pink later told VH1 that she got into a disagreement with the trainer over the scene. "I could see how painful it was for it to get down on its hands and knees, and I'm like, 'Can we not do this any more? I think we got the take, you know, it's enough.'"

Several years later, Pink once again invoked her uncomfortable experience with the elephant on the video set in a letter to the Las Vegas performers Siegfried & Roy. "The poor soul was more tense and uncomfortable than I would be in *The Mickey Mouse Club*," Pink wrote, as part of a heartfelt plea in which she implored the duo to let their elephant, Gildah, live in a wildlife sanctuary. "In a sanctuary, Gildah could forage through hundreds of acres of lush vegetation, play in the pond and at least have some life as nature intended ... Sure beats life in a tiny tourist trap."

It's understandable that Pink might be seen as hypocritical for being so pro-animal rights and yet still agreeing to take part in a video featuring an elephant. In 2003, she acknowledged this disconnect in a handwritten letter to *Vogue*, detailing a request that the magazine stop pushing the wearing of fur. "I would like to say I've always been fur-free," she wrote. "Unfortunately, I went through a selfish phase and wore fur on a couple of occasions." Pink went on to add that now she "wouldn't be seen dead in the stuff" due to the treatment animals on fur farms experienced.

Pink didn't censor herself when talking to royalty, either. "I was happy to hear that I was your first choice to play at your 21st birthday bash," Pink wrote to Prince William in 2003, "then disgusted to learn that you hunt and kill animals for fun." She then described the graphic way the prince allegedly killed a deer. "Why? Was it some kind of 'trying to prove you're a man' trip?" She was even more graphic in 2006 while criticizing Kentucky Fried Chicken's (KFC) cooking practices, after seeing a PETA exposé. "We're simply asking KFC to modernize its methods," Pink said.

Left: Animal-lover Pink arrives with her dog to 2001's MTV Movie Awards

Opposite: Pink stars in a PETA campaign promoting a fur-free nightclub, in New York City

"The only wildlife at Centro-Fly is human.
No fur coats allowed."
—P!nk
CENTRO-FLY HELPS YOU
45 W. 21st St., NYC
FurIsDead.com
PETA
Photo: Terry Richardson

Right: Pink's performance at 2019's Brit Awards culminates in a powerful and political take on "What About Us"

In the years since, Pink has thrown her weight behind countless social and political issues involved with animal rights and other concerns. For example, in 2006 she supported the development of a mobile vet service that could spay and neuter stray dogs and cats. "It breaks my heart," she said. "I want to take them all home, but I can't. I'd have 350,000 dogs if I did." In 2015, she took part in PETA's "I'd rather go naked than wear fur" campaign, posing for a photo that ran in Times Square as a ninety-foot billboard.

Pink has also put her money where her mouth is. Over the years, she's donated to hurricane relief efforts and wildfire recovery funds, as well as supported notable organizations such as the Human Rights Campaign, ONE Campaign, The Prince's Trust, Save the Children, Take Back the Night, and Run for the Cure Foundation. She's been an outspoken supporter of LGBTQ rights and same-sex marriage; has supported Ukrainians affected by the war that began in 2022 by promoting UNICEF's efforts and spoke out in favor of gun control.

In 2021, when members of the Norwegian women's beach handball team were fined €1,500 after wearing shorts like the men's team—instead of bikini bottoms—Pink even offered to pony up for their fine. "I'm VERY proud of the Norwegian female beach handball team FOR PROTESTING THE VERY SEXIST RULES ABOUT THEIR 'uniform,'" she tweeted, adding, "Good on ya, ladies. I'll be happy to pay your fines for you. Keep it up." As it turns out, Pink is as generous as she is talented—and isn't afraid to use her voice and platform to help those in need.

She affirmed this once again in June 2022, after the US Supreme Court overturned Roe v. Wade, which removed national protections for US abortion access. Pink went viral after tweeting, "Let's be clear: If you believe the government belongs in a woman's uterus, a gay persons business or marriage, or that racism is okay- THEN PLEASE IN THE NAME OF YOUR LORD NEVER FUCKING LISTEN TO MY MUSIC AGAIN." The following month, Pink released "Irrelevant,"—a protest song highlighting the continued fight for women's rights, and addressing the online hate Pink received after voicing her opinion about the issue—making it clear that she isn't afraid to stand up for what she believes.

LOVE REVOLUTION
JUSTICE
LGBT
FIGHT LESBIAN AND GAY OPPRESSION
NO HUMAN BEING IS ILLEGAL
HUMAN RIGHTS
POWER TO THE PEOPLE
EVERY HUMAN HAS RIGHTS
FREEDOM OF EXPRESSION
WE DEMAND EQUALITY NOT YOUR APPROVAL
LOVE FOR ALL
WE DEMAND IT
#PEOPLE
IS THE ANSWER
CLIMATE CHANGE IS REAL

MISSUNDAZTOOD

"Pink had an amazing tone; she sounded like Joplin on steroids. She brought such a broad paintbrush in her vocal tone."

RON FAIR

In early 2001, Pink was still riding a wave of momentum from the success of her debut album, *Can't Take Me Home*. She performed "Most Girls" at the American Music Awards on January 8. Although it wasn't her greatest performance—her voice had a wobbly edge and wasn't as powerful as usual—the appearance signaled a new era. Gone was the magenta hair and baggy, sporty clothing. Instead, she wore a smartly tailored, flared-leg, white suit over a black snakeskin bodysuit. She paired them with a black bandit mask and a messy mop of platinum-blonde hair.

Can't Take Me Home's third single, "You Make Me Sick," was also starting its ascent on the pop and R&B charts in the US and UK, aided by a surreal music video directed by Pink's frequent collaborator Dave Meyers. In a nod to the song's lyrics, which describe the dangerous lure of an illicit crush, the clip depicts the volatile relationship between Pink and an on-screen boyfriend. At one point, he tosses a piece of flaming firewood in her direction; it shatters a chandelier, which prompts the couple to have a contrite reconciliation and then a rare moment of romantic connection. At another moment, the pair end up running a red light while fighting and get into a huge accident; in fact, they keep bickering while spinning around upside down in their bright-pink car.

To add levity, Pink is frequently shown luxuriating in a pool of flowers, with strategically placed petals over sensitive areas of her body, a sly reference to the movie *American Beauty*. Pink told *NME* that a lot of the video's ideas—such as another memorable moment where she perches on the lap of a mall Santa—came from her. "We get to make a lot of fun videos. This one was the most stress-relieving. All that glass you see break? I got to do that every take. I had more glass, every take. I'm like, 'I could get used to this!'"

"You Make Me Sick" reached the UK Top Ten in late January and the US Top Forty in February. However, Pink was soon about to see her career move up to an entirely different level thanks to a movie soundtrack. Director Baz Luhrmann and his music team had decided Labelle's 1974 No. 1 hit "Lady Marmalade" was perfect for his movie *Moulin Rouge*. The song ended up being used prominently in the script, its come-hither premise serving as the perfect backdrop for the grand entrance of French courtesans.

However, Luhrmann had an even grander plan for "Lady Marmalade" outside of the movie. "Because the Moulin Rouge had such diversity, my original idea was, 'Let's do "Lady Marmalade," but let's let all of the characters be sung by the greatest pop singers from each continent in the world,'" he told *Billboard*. Although if anyone could pull off such a gambit it would be Luhrmann, he added that the movie's music supervisor, Laura Wasserman, brought him back down to earth. "[She told me] 'Look, that sounds like it'll take forever to do. Why don't we go with every different genre in America? Let's get the most emerging pop singer, the edgiest rap artist ...'"

That concept was much more feasible. Eventually, a "Lady Marmalade" remake coalesced around an impressive crew: rapper Lil' Kim, R&B star Mýa, pop icon Christina Aguilera and Pink. For good measure, the song was co-produced by hip-hop visionary Missy Elliott and her collaborator Rockwilder, with vocals

Previous: Performing "Most Girls" onstage at the 28th Annual American Music Awards, January 8, 2001, at the Shrine Auditorium in Los Angeles

Opposite: (L-R): Christina Aguilera, Mýa, Patti LaBelle, Pink, and Lil' Kim at the 44th Annual Grammy Awards, Los Angeles, February 27, 2002

Right: Performing "Lady Marmalade" from the *Moulin Rouge* movie soundtrack, at 2001's MTV Movie Awards. (L-R): Pink, Lil' Kim, Mýa, and Christina Aguilera.

produced by Ron Fair. The women largely recorded their parts separately due to busy schedules. Even so, the results were impressive. In fact, it became clear Pink was brought in specifically to bring a rock edge, as what she sang brought a smoky, edgy timbre to her vocals.

Ron Fair who had signed Aguilera to her record deal and also mentored her, told *Billboard*, "Pink had an amazing tone; she sounded like Joplin on steroids. She brought such a broad paintbrush in her vocal tone." Added Rockwilder, "There are a lot of things that a lot of people don't know Pink is capable of vocally, man—she does it effortlessly. She'll do it with a beer and a cigarette in her hand, you know?"

Everyone was able to gather in person for the "Lady Marmalade" video shoot. The colorful clip was of a piece with *Moulin Rouge* the movie, both in its rich set design and elaborate costumes. Pink's look especially stood out. In one scene, she sports curly, pink-streaked hair, as well as a gigantic rhinestone necklace, a pink bra and a copper-colored corset. In another scene, she struts her stuff while wearing a top hat with a glittering "P" on it, a sparkly bra and delicate patterned stockings held up by garters. Yet, as she confessed to E! News in 2021, "I was not happy about my outfit. Yeah, I did not want to be in booty shorts, but I got into it. Cameras started rolling, and I started feeling myself." The benefit of hindsight also softened her stance, as she added, "Now I look at it, I'm like, 'Oh, my god, that body. Why didn't I appreciate it?'"

Pink and Christina Aguilera also reportedly did not get along on the video set, a clash that ended up being tabloid fodder for years. Tina Landon, the video's lead choreographer, told *Cosmopolitan*, "These are four big, individual, lots-of-personality artists in one room at one time at the height of their careers

Below left: The MTV Music Video Awards, September 6, 2001. Pink, Lil' Kim and Christina Aguilera scoop Video of the Year and Best Video from a Film for "Lady Marmalade."

Opposite: Former 4 Non Blondes lead singer and songwriter Linda Perry pictured in her recording studio in 2005

... I think it's pretty public knowledge that there was tension between Christina and Pink." According to Pink herself, that tension may have developed well before the filming. On an episode of *Behind the Music*, she alleged that Ron Fair played favorites as the song came together giving preference to mentee Aguilera. Recalling a meeting about the song with the executive, Pink said, "He didn't say 'hi' to any of us and said, 'What's the high part? What's the most singing part? Christina's going to take that part,'" adding that she strenuously objected to this arrangement.

However, any bad feelings between the women dissolved along with time. Pink revealed on a 2017 episode of a talk show called *Watch What Happens Live with Andy Cohen* that she and Aguilera made up after crossing paths on talent show *The Voice*, bonding over having grown and changed. "We were super-young and super-new at the whole thing, and I think I'm an alpha, and she's an alpha," Pink said candidly. "I'm used to taking my altercations physical, and she's used to having them verbal. We're just very different." She also pointed out the sexism inherent in the idea that women are often at odds. "Women have to learn how to support each other. It's not taught to each other in the playground."

Despite the rocky genesis, the "Lady Marmalade" video was an immediate success. On April 16, the clip debuted on the MTV *TRL* countdown at No. 5. "Lady Marmalade" also quickly became a pop hit. In June, the song reached No. 1 on the *Billboard* Hot 100, where it would spend five weeks. The song also topped the charts in Germany, Ireland, Australia, and the UK.

In a neat coincidence, on the same day the song topped the *Billboard* Hot 100 singles chart, Pink joined collaborators Christina Aguilera, Lil' Kim and Mýa at the MTV Movie Awards and performed "Lady

"When I got together with her, I just had a feeling. My instinct said, 'Don't go and be an artist again, don't go and get another record deal ... investigate this girl and find out what you can do with her.'"

LINDA PERRY

Marmalade" on an elaborate set that mirrored the movie's vibe. The staging and performance ended up giving each woman in the song a chance to shine. Pink showed none of the nerves she did at the American Music Awards. She strode to the front of the stage and belted out her part while reprising the outfit she wore in the video. Her increased confidence was palpable.

Months later, the women were also big winners at the MTV Video Music Awards, as "Lady Marmalade" won Video of the Year and Best Video from a Film. And on February 27, 2002, Pink won her first Grammy Award when "Lady Marmalade" took Best Pop Collaboration with Vocals. It wouldn't be her last major award—especially as her second album, *M!ssundaztood*, was in stores.

Pink was ready for a change after *Can't Take Me Home*. She certainly had the vocal chops needed for R&B success and the thick-skinned attitude needed to become a major pop star. However, she longed to have more control over her look and music. "I loved *Can't Take Me Home*," she told the *Los Angeles Times*. "The only thing I didn't like was I didn't have a say. Back then in Atlanta, it wasn't about the artist. It was about the producer and especially new artists." As she put it to *The Face*, *Can't Take Me Home* "wasn't mine. I didn't get to push all the buttons."

Pink decided to take charge of her creative destiny when it came to putting together her next full-length record. She loved the rock band 4 Non Blondes, who had a major hit in 1993 with the soaring song "What's Up?" but broke up after releasing one album. She especially admired the group's lead singer, Linda Perry, and decided a musical collaboration was in order. With a little ingenuity, Pink tracked Perry down, digging out the musician's phone number from the book of her makeup artist, Billy Brasfield. "I left her a ten-minute message about how much I loved her and how she owes me because I got arrested singing her music out of my window at 3.30 in the morning, and how I'm gonna stalk her if she doesn't return my call," Pink told *Rolling Stone* in 2002. "She called back five minutes later and said, 'You're fuckin' crazy – you should come over.'"

At the time, Perry was rekindling her solo career, and was in the process of booking live showcases in hopes of landing a record deal. In an interview with the website HitQuarters, Perry even admitted she had "no idea" who Pink was before the "weird phone call" seeking a collaboration. "She was this white girl singing R&B music, and it made absolutely no sense to me why she would call me."

However, Perry changed course after meeting Pink, canceling proposed label showcases and turning her attention to the eager young singer. "When I got together with her, I just had a feeling. My instinct said, 'Don't go and be an artist again, don't go and get another record deal ... investigate this girl and find out what you can do with her.'"

Perry's excitement stemmed from the connection the pair made; they quickly started making music together. As Pink recalled to *Rolling Stone*, any initial awkwardness melted away quickly. She grabbed a microphone as Perry took to the piano, and they wrote the first song for the album, "Eventually," in about five minutes. That was the start of a fruitful period: Pink and Perry wrote twenty songs together over the next month and a half. "I just didn't leave," Pink said. "I camped out on her furry rug."

The songs from these sessions emphasized Pink's strengths: vocals from the heart and vulnerable lyrics, rooted in her real-life dramas. "Eventually" is a low-lit, introspective ballad criticizing people who use Pink for her fame or take advantage of her good nature, while the hazy "Going to California" is about her discovery that the grass wasn't necessarily greener when she left Philadelphia for the West Coast. Other songs find Pink processing her family traumas. "Dear Diary," which boasts an acoustic guitar loop with a psychedelic twist, is a brutally honest song in which Pink references her parents' divorce and her own troublesome behavior. "My Vietnam" is also sobering, as she compares her life experiences to the Vietnam War.

Pink told *Rolling Stone* of Perry, "She became a really, really good friend and I treasure her. You don't meet a lot of people in L.A. who are so raw and honest."

Not every Perry-Pink collaboration was sobering and serious, however. The retro-funky "Respect" is a female empowerment anthem nodding to Aretha Franklin's song of the same name. And *M!ssundaztood*'s first single, "Get the Party Started," is a rainbow-hued burst of colorful grooves and raucous lyrics that's ideal for pre-gaming before a big night out.

"Get the Party Started" emerged from experimentation. Perry was hanging out with a friend talking music, she told *Tape Op* in 2021. "I said, 'Hey, what's that crazy bad sound that's all over the radio right now?'" The friend identified the Korg Triton keyboard and an Akai drum programmer called an MPC. "[They told me]

Opposite: Music manager Roger Davies (left) pictured in 1985 with Cher and Tina Turner at an MTV awards party

'You can put drum sounds in it on a disc, and you can get different kicks and snares. You program your own beats.'" Intrigued by the new technology, Perry bought the popular equipment and the software ProTools and started trying to figure out how everything worked by making beats, layering bass and finding a groove.

Almost accidentally, she created the foundation of "Get the Party Started," long before Pink became involved. "I was having so much fun, so I grabbed a harmonica microphone and started ad-libbing, 'I'm coming up, so you better get this party started,'" Perry shared. "I started thinking of every cliché thing that I could say, and that was the song. Then I started laughing, going, 'Holy fuck, I wrote a dance hit!'" Perry might have the sole writing credit, but it's Pink's celebratory attitude that makes the song hers. Her delivery make it clear she's raring to attend a wild rager—and she's expecting to have the biggest blast *ever* when she rolls up.

Perry wasn't the only collaborator that helped Pink move her career forward circa *M!ssundaztood*. She also teamed up with manager Roger Davies, who had also overseen the careers of Cher, Tina Turner and Sade. "I basically convinced him to take me on," she told *Variety*. "I told him that I wanted to be a touring artist and that I wanted to be a f–king legend. And he was like: 'OK,

you f—king crazy little brat. Let's do this!' That was the first great decision I made."

Davies not only intuitively understood Pink—"I could immediately see that she had her own clear vision of who she wanted to be and where she wanted to go," he said in 2019—he helped get her business affairs in order, starting with her lopsided record deal. "He looked at the contract and he was like: 'What the f–k did you do?'" Pink later recalled. "I was like, 'I don't know but I got a catsuit!' I mean, it's ridiculous looking back on it now, but it got me from A to B."

Creatively, Pink also connected with the songwriter/producer Dallas Austin, who was known for his work with Boyz II Men, After 7 and Madonna. "She came to me and she was literally sitting on the steps in the front of my studios," Austin told Songwriter Universe. "And she said, 'I'm not leaving until you work with me.'" Pink's outfit at the time—a silk jacket and roller skates—reminded Austin of tough-girl character Pinky Tuscadero from the TV show *Happy Days*. As a result, their collaborations also helped cement Pink as someone who confronted life's messier moments.

Take the rock-leaning "Just Like a Pill," which employs an extended metaphor comparing an unsatisfying romantic partner to illegal substances. Pink drew on her wilder younger days for lyrical inspiration, she shared with the *Los Angeles Times*. "The first thing that comes to mind with this? When I used to be on drugs, I should write a song about it. When you're young, you think your ideas are so clever." Austin, meanwhile, says his inspiration was a fraught relationship with an ex, which he channeled almost verbatim into the song's lyrics. "We were out there taking pills that made you feel good," he shared, "and when we broke up, instead of that pill making me feel better, it made me feel ill."

Another Austin co-write, "Don't Let Me Get Me," was also about tumult. Pink referenced taboo

Opposite: Pink as Dina Dexter alongside Tracy Morgan as Grand Master Freddy in *Saturday Night Live* skit , "The Shout-Out Show," January 2002

behavior (dating teachers), teenage rebellion (parental disagreements) and feelings of self-loathing as supporting evidence for why she wished she was someone else. More notably, "Don't Let Me Get Me" features a lyrical reference to Britney Spears that was widely misunderstood as a critique. In reality, Pink was praising Spears' looks and demeanor, and lamented she herself could never compete with the " ... Baby One More Time" singer.

The Spears reference became an interview talking point for years; one 2004 interview even described Britney as Pink's "arch-rival." This kind of comparison wasn't out of the ordinary: During this era, the press often positioned female pop stars against one another, as if only one could be in the spotlight at once. For example, Spears was also frequently compared to her fellow former *Mickey Mouse Club* cast member Christina Aguilera. Pink herself became known for fanning these competitive flames, telling *The Mirror* in 2004, she performed "real music" and sang live instead of "mim[ing] to a track" during live shows. "I feel like shaking some of these girls up who have forgotten what it means to actually sing for their fans. I may swear and be boisterous and make people angry, but nobody can accuse me of not being true to the fans."

Decades later, with the benefit of hindsight and maturity, Pink had the perspective to see how damaging these comparisons could be. "It was so unfair to all the girls," she told *People* in 2021. "None of us wanted that." Pink stressed that she especially had no issues with Spears—and reiterated that the two women were vastly different. "I love Britney — she used to carry around my album," she continued. "I was like, 'Dude, I'm a street punk, I just skateboard. That doesn't have to be the anti-Britney. I don't want to fight anybody.'"

This revisionist perspective also extended to her music; years later, speaking to the *Los Angeles Times* about "Don't Let Me Get Me," she quipped, "I wish I could burn that song and never sing it again." Back in 2001, however, this song's sound and attitude helped convince her label that Pink was on to something special with her rocker persona. "When I started working with Pink, I would play the songs for L.A. Reid, but he didn't like them at first," Austin says, "but then a few weeks later he said, 'You know what? This stuff is great. Finish doing what you're doing.' And so then we did 'Don't Let Me Get Me.'"

Austin wasn't the only one who had to convince Reid to get onboard with the rock-edged musical vision. Pink herself was vocal about the challenges she faced being true to herself once she became a solo artist. "It's been fun fighting with [Reid] over the past six years because I always win," she told *Rolling Stone*. More specifically, Pink said her "outspokenness and my eating manners" rankled some at her label. In particular, the way she approached her food at an expensive industry event featuring an $8,000-a-plate dinner especially turned heads for all the wrong reasons.

"The next day I got a call from the label asking me to take etiquette classes," Pink said. "They tried to convince me that it's better to know the rules and then break them. I said, 'If I know them and break them, I'll just have a guilt trip.'" She did give in to label requests and try media coaching, although that also wasn't successful. "They wanted to teach me to be diplomatic, to give journalists the answers they want, and I'm like, 'Wouldn't you rather have the truth?'" she told *The Guardian*. "The only thing I know how to say is what I feel."

As it turned out, Pink's insistence on being true to herself—and being honest—paid off big time. Lead

Opposite: Steven Tyler and Pink performing at 2002's KIIS FM Wango Tango, Rose Bowl, Pasadena, California

single "Get the Party Started" was a global sensation, topping the singles charts in Australia, Ireland, New Zealand, Belgium, and Spain, and hitting No. 2 in Germany, Switzerland and the UK. In a sign of the song's crossover appeal, "Get the Party Started" also topped the *Billboard* Hot Dance Music Club Play chart. "Don't Let Me Get Me" and "Just Like a Pill" were also wildly successful: Both singles reached the Top Ten around the world, while the latter hit No. 1 in the UK. Released in November 2001, the album *M!ssundaztood* too ended up a smash, reaching the Top Ten in the US, Austria, New Zealand, and Canada. In the UK, the album reached No. 2, kept from the top spot only by Avril Lavigne's *Let Go*.

Emboldened by this chart success, she was the musical guest on the long-running comedy show *Saturday Night Live* in late January 2002. Wearing pale-pink hair extensions that cascaded down her back like a pastel waterfall, she performed two songs: a funkier version of "Get the Party Started" and a churning, rock-oriented take on "Don't Let Me Get Me." She also stretched her acting chops, portraying an outrageous character on a skit called "The Shout-Out Show."

As with *Can't Take Me Home*, *M!ssundaztood* benefitted from music videos that put Pink in the spotlight. She revisited her comfort zone and turned to Dave Meyers for the neon-hued "Get the Party Started," which appropriately showed off a more playful side of Pink's personality. The video starts with her getting ready to go to a party, and trying on different outfits before settling on an orange fishnet shirt over a white camisole, low-slung pants that expose her underwear, and a spiky hairdo. Pink and a friend jump into a convertible, ready to start the night, but are forced to hop on skateboards to get to the club after running out of gas. Denied entrance, they sneak in anyway and saunter to the bar just in time to grab a drink and then participate in a dance-off.

Meyers also directed the "Don't Let Me Get Me" video, which ended up a lighthearted and inspiring read of the song's autobiographical lyrics. Pink stars as a misfit high-school student who wishes she was anyone but herself; at one point, she's even taunted by her own image in the mirror. As the video unfolds, Pink tries on different personas—including a curly-haired pop ingenue and a glammed-up star with hair that is cockatoo-like in its majesty—before finding her comfort zone fronting a rock band at her high school reunion.

In contrast, "Just Like a Pill" introduced a darker—even gothic—edge to Pink's look. She sported raven-colored hair and an all-black outfit as she writhed on the ground and acted out the song's angst. "All my videos have been very cartoony," she told VH1. "This one's very dark and artsy, and I have black hair, which is very fun. I loved it."

Pink's rocker side translated to her live shows. In 2000, she noted in multiple interviews that she most wished to collaborate with Aerosmith frontman Steven Tyler. That dream came true on *M!ssundaztood*, as Tyler contributed vocals to the bluesy torch song "Misery." (In another wish-come-true, the song also featured Bon Jovi's Richie Sambora on guitar.) Tyler later joined Pink to perform the song at the June 2002 Wango Tango concert in front of thousands of people at the Rose Bowl. The pair stood center-stage, matching each other note for wailing note on the smoldering song, as the crowd cheered wildly. Fittingly, directly before the pair's duet, Pink got herself into hard rock mode by performing a passionate, faithful cover of Aerosmith's 1990 hit "Janie's Got a Gun."

In summer 2002, Pink opened for rocker Lenny Kravitz's summer tour. Supporting a big superstar is difficult no matter how talented you are, which Pink admitted in an interview with VH1. "There are not as many people [in the audience] that dress up like me," she said, describing the differences between being a headliner and opener. "It's very easy to perform in front of screaming young girls. But when you kind of have to win people over, it's a little more work. But it's fun; it's challenging." Ever savvy, she pulled out some of her most rock-oriented tricks—including a Janis Joplin cover—to engage the crowd.

The accolades kept rolling in as the year progressed. In August, Pink won two MTV Video Music Awards for "Get the Party Started," in the categories of Best Dance Video and Best Female Video. She notoriously accepted the latter award from Avril Lavigne and Lisa Marie Presley by quipping, "I'm too drunk for this." (Perhaps that's why the version of "Just Like a Pill" she performed on the show was especially heavy, nodding to the video's moody visuals and channeling a grimy punk show.) "Get the Party Started" also won Best Song at the MTV Europe Music Awards.

By fall 2002, *M!ssundaztood* was also still going strong. Pink released her fourth and final single from the album, "Family Portrait." Adapted from a poem she wrote at age nine, around the time of her parents' split, the song was heartwrenching. Unsurprisingly, the song poured out of her in the studio in just twenty minutes, an avalanche of emotion and memory about her turbulent family life. "I was crying [after the song was done]," she told *The Face*. "And I felt so naked and vulnerable and horrible and spent, I just left. I had to leave." In fact, "Family Portrait" was even difficult for her to listen to in the studio. "I just couldn't let people know that much about me, and me be there while they were listening to it."

"They wanted to teach me to be diplomatic, to give journalists the answers they want, and I'm like, 'Wouldn't you rather have the truth?'"

Right: Pink onstage at the 2002 MTV Video Music Awards, at Radio City Music Hall, in New York City

> "I thought if I wrote those songs that would be it and I'd never have to talk about it again, but it was the exact opposite. Every interview was a therapy session, and after two years I was done."

Fittingly, the "Family Portrait" video was also quite moving. Helmed by award-winning director Sophie Muller, who was known for her work with No Doubt, Annie Lennox and Blur, the clip stars Pink and a child actress who represents Pink's younger self. The juxtaposition is striking: The younger girl plays up how emotional it was growing up in a tumultuous household, as the real Pink takes it all in and reacts. At one point, adult Pink comforts her younger self, a touching display of solidarity loaded with meaning.

"Family Portrait" peaked at No. 20 on the *Billboard* Hot 100 in early 2003, becoming the fourth song from the album to reach the Top Forty and Pink's eighth straight Top Forty song. Over the years, Pink has described receiving letters from fans, describing what "Family Portrait" means to them. It's not the only song of hers to speak to other people in such a profound way, but it did embody the transformative nature of her honesty.

"I started to realize that when I am the most uncomfortable and the most vulnerable and saying the most honest, shameful shit, that's what's getting to somebody else," she told *The Guardian* in 2017. "And I'm basically having therapy and somebody else is getting something from it. That's the only thing that was meaningful to me. I didn't care about winning awards or being on the cover of magazines or people liking me."

In an interview at the time with VH1, Pink said it wasn't difficult being so personal. "No, because I don't know how to keep my own secrets ... It's hard, after the fact, when everybody knows everything about you, and you're like, 'Damn, I shouldn't have said that.' But I don't think about it at the time. I think it's good because the deeper inside you go, the more you're related to somebody else, because life is life – everybody goes through the same things."

Pink's open-book approach did take a heavy toll, even if she didn't realize it right away. Much later, she admitted that having to talk about her deeply personal songs over and over (and over) again dredged up painful memories in a way that could be emotionally draining. "I thought if I wrote those songs that would be it and I'd never have to talk about it again, but it was the exact opposite," she told the *Los Angeles Times*. "It was, 'So tell me about [your parents'] divorce.' Every interview was a therapy session, and after two years I was done."

When Pink says she's done or has reached the end of the line with something, she means it. And so, much as with *Can't Take Me Home*, after the *M!ssundaztood* promotion cycle wound down, Pink changed up her look and sound once again. Gone was the super-confessional songwriter. In her place was a rebellious punk ready to let loose and smash musical boundaries.

Opposite: Pink with her Best Female Video Award at 2002's MTV Video Music Awards

TRY THIS

When Pink sat down for an interview with ABC's *Primetime Live* before the release of her third studio album, *Try This*, host Diane Sawyer used the now familiar talking point that Pink was a rebellious outsider different from other pop stars. "She is not Britney, not Christina, not Beyoncé—and that's the way Pink likes it. With twelve million album sales and some serious attitude, she does everything her way and won't be told, especially by guys in suits, what to do."

Although Pink wasn't trying to model herself after her peers, the idea that she followed her own muse rang true. That's been a hallmark of Pink's entire career—but it was especially true after the success of *M!ssundaztood*. Despite the album's runaway success, she declined to replicate its sonic formula. Instead, Pink ripped up her rulebook (again).

"I have no intention of making [*Try This*] just as big [as *M!ssundaztood*]," she told MTV. "I'd love just as many people to hear it, and of course there's pressure, but you just can't work under those circumstances. I can't live like that."

Pink made it clear she was changing things up with her February 2003 performance at the Brit Awards. In a move straight out of The Sex Pistols' anti-royalty playbook, she rose out onto the stage from an upside-down crown amid a crowd of stoic palace guards. Sporting

"I've always been very rebellious. My dad was a rebellious person, and I was raised that way. That's what punk rock is: freedom to do whatever you want."

Previous: In concert at the Birmingham NEC, England, UK, 2004

Opposite, above: At a press conference for new album *Try This*, The Langham, London, UK, 2003

Right: Pink emerges onstage from a giant crown flanked by dancers dressed as British palace guards, at the Brit Awards, 2003

Right: Filming the music video for "Feel Good Time," a song that appears on movie soundtrack, *Charlie's Angels: Full Throttle*

a dark magenta mohawk and bright-yellow pants, she and a live band ripped through a hardcore-influenced "Get the Party Started," which provoked the guards to shed their formal gear and transform into punks. She also sped through "Just Like a Pill," commanding the stage with confidence and urgency.

Pink's new studio direction was apparent in the song "Feel Good Time," which arrived in 2003 as part of the *Charlie's Angels: Full Throttle* movie and soundtrack. Produced by William Orbit, who also co-wrote the song with Beck, "Feel Good Time" had a decidedly synth-pop sound that sampled Spirit's "Fresh-Garbage" and softened Pink's recent sound. The single didn't duplicate the runaway success of "Lady Marmalade" in America—except for the dance charts, where it reached the Top Ten—but it was a huge summer jam in the UK and Australia.

When it came time to *Try This*, Pink once again wrote songs with Linda Perry. Circumstances were slightly different this time around. For starters, Perry was now an in-demand studio collaborator thanks not just to the success of *M!ssundaztood*, but also because she wrote and produced Christina Aguilera's Grammy-winning 2002 ballad "Beautiful." Perry and Pink decamped to Pink's house with a twenty-four-track recorder. "It's so not what anybody's gonna expect from her," Perry told MTV in May 2003 of the new music. "It shows the artist in her. She's definitely reached a whole 'nother level of musicianship."

The songs Pink and Perry worked on were creative leaps forward. "Catch Me While I'm Sleeping" is an R&B slow jam throwback, while "Waiting for Love" is a strident acoustic rock jam that hints at Led Zeppelin and other, heavy, seventies' folk-rockers. "Try Too Hard," meanwhile, is a ripping rocker that rages against conformity and fake people.

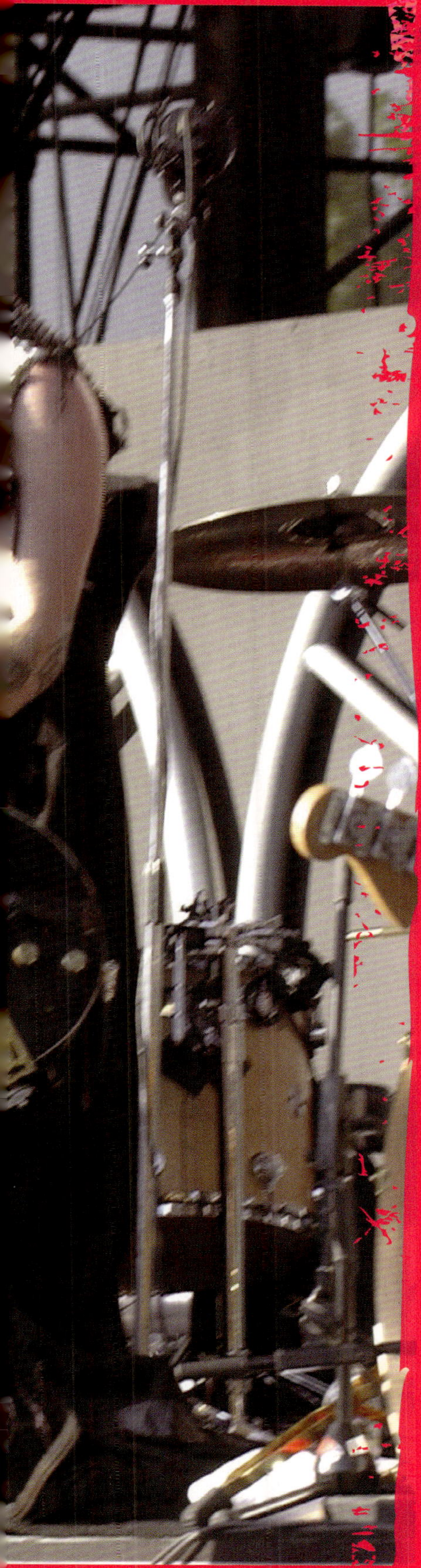

"All I know is that if people are gonna give me shit for working with the best woman vocalist in the world right now, then let them give me shit. Pink is the shit, and working with her has been all positive."

TIM ARMSTRONG, RANCID

"Try Hard" embodies the ways *Try This* threw listeners a curveball, finding Pink embracing her love for punk rock. By the early 2000s, punk had evolved well beyond its roots as a raucous musical rebellion—and Pink understood intuitively that it was as much a mindset as it was a music subculture. "I've always been very rebellious," Pink told *NME* in 2001. "My dad was a rebellious person, and I was raised that way. That's what punk rock is: freedom to do whatever you want." Pink teased this new direction (and showed off her punk bona fides) in June 2003 during a surprise cameo at the KROQ Weenie Roast, the high-profile annual concert staged by the California alternative rock radio station. The vocalist teamed up with the Transplants, a supergroup featuring Rancid's Tim Armstrong and blink-182's Travis Barker, to perform the band's "Weigh on My Mind" and a revved-up take on her own hit, "Get the Party Started."

This performance presaged the anything-goes approach of *Try This*, which featured nine songs co-written and produced by Armstrong and drums from Barker. Despite Pink's rock background and recent

Left: Pink performing onstage with The Transplants during 2003's KROQ Weenie Roast, Verizon Amphitheater, California, June 14, 2003

Right: Pink on the set of her music video for "Trouble," 2003

collaborations with Perry, the pairing with Armstrong was still head-scratching. He was a Bay Area music legend, first with the ska-punk icons Operation Ivy and then with the raucous punk band Rancid; the latter was enormously popular starting in the nineties. Back in 2003, it was also still somewhat unexpected (if not odd) for pop and rock worlds to collide. For example, when Liz Phair released a self-titled album that year which sounded far different from her guitar-heavy nineties albums, she was roundly criticized.

At this time, Pink and Armstrong also ran in different circles. Rancid was a major attraction on touring punk festival the Vans Warped Tour in 2001 when Pink was burning up the *Billboard* pop charts with "Lady Marmalade." However, the musicians hit it off immediately, with Armstrong telling MTV he considered Pink like a sister. "I was like, 'Yo, this is my homegirl. If I grew up with you, I'd roll with you. You'd be my girl,'" he said, while adding that he saw nothing strange about their collaboration. "All I know is that if people are gonna give me shit for working with the best woman vocalist in the world right now, then let them give me shit. Pink is the shit, and working with her has been all positive."

Pink also had nothing but positive things to say about teaming up with a tattoo-heavy, leather-jacket-wearing punk rocker to make pop music. Armstrong was a supportive presence in the studio who gave her votes of confidence and was enthusiastic about her musical direction. "He was like this burst of energy," Pink told MTV. "And he's really good for your ego, having him around, because everything you do, he's like, 'That's amazing!' 'What do you think of this melody?' 'That's rad!'"

As she did with her *M!ssundaztood* writing sessions with Perry, Pink went all in on her collaboration with Armstrong. She hopped on a tour the Transplants did with Foo Fighters and grabbed a bunk on the bus. "[We] set up drums in the hallway and guitars in the back and ProTools, and we recorded three songs on the bus in two days," she told MTV.

Overall, she and Armstrong wrote ten songs in just two weeks. It was clear their talents complemented one another. "We could just sit down and my voice would be all fucked up, and she would sing like an angel," Armstrong told MTV. "She can stack, like, five harmonies real quick. She's a very talented singer and a very talented lyricist."

Alongside Armstrong, *Try This* boasted an eclectic, all-star cast of musical collaborators. John Fields—who would later go on to produce Jonas Brothers, Miley Cyrus, and Demi Lovato—contributed a variety of instrumental colors, while future Oscar-winner Atticus Ross and beloved cult musician Matt Mahaffey added synths and percussion. On the rock side, Armstrong's Rancid bandmates Matt Freeman and Brett Reed added rhythmic heft, while Steve Stevens, a hard-rock guitarist known for his work with Billy Idol, contributed his iconic instrumental work.

With so much talent aboard, it was perhaps inevitable that *Try This* wouldn't necessarily end up being a straightforward punk album. While songs such as "Humble Neighborhoods" and "Trouble" are indebted to snarling aggression, other tunes expand Pink's sound in even more interesting directions. Horns pepper the ska-kissed "Tonight's The Night" and soul-influenced "Walk Away," while the sixties' rock throwback "Unwind" puts Pink's smoky, bluesy snarl at the forefront. The slinky, cinematic "Oh My God," which was co-written by and features the Canadian electro-rock

Opposite: Pink plays Wembley Arena, UK, March 23, 2004

act Peaches, is a song brimming with extended lyrical metaphors about a hot and heavy seduction.

In a way, the *Try This* era was Pink fulfilling a teenage dream of being in a band, which she always perceived to be the height of fun. "A bunch of friends traveling cross-country in a van, broke as shit, getting to each venue on skateboards, laughing and joking and having the time of your life," she told *Blender* in 2002. "It's all I ever wanted." But *Try This* was also a deliberate step back from the intense and confessional approach to *M!ssundaztood*.

"It was really fast, really easy. There was no resistance with this album," she told MTV News. "[Making *M!ssundaztood*] was enlightening and liberating and powerful and lyrical, and blah, blah, blah. It's emotionally draining to be that naked and that vulnerable. I didn't have a plan [for the new album]. I just knew I wanted to have fun and I didn't want to complain all the time."

But even if *Try This* wasn't overtly personal, that doesn't necessarily mean the album is lighthearted. The acoustic ballad "Love Song" is "definitely more about fear than the average 'I love you, I found you, I'm going to be with you for the rest of my life,'" she told MTV News. "It's more based on the fear that comes along with loving someone." And "Unwind" is a bittersweet song written from the perspective of Janis Joplin; the song hints at loneliness, references her love of Southern Comfort and alludes to the fact her life ended at age twenty-seven.

Once again, Pink's label head, L.A. Reid, wasn't necessarily fully convinced about the change in direction on *Try This*, although he told *The Guardian* there wasn't necessarily any "conflict" over the sound. "I just wanted to make sure she covered her core fanbase from the first album. She is a rapidly evolving artist. She can sing like Janis Joplin, she's got the edge and the range. I will be interested to see how *Try This* does."

In America, the album started on a good note. Released on November 11, 2003, it debuted at No. 9 on the *Billboard* Top 200, selling 147,000 copies its first week, and was certified platinum in mid-December. Pink was also the musical guest on *Saturday Night Live* to promote the album. Unfortunately, this didn't translate to lasting commercial success. *Try This* only spent fifteen weeks on the US Billboard album charts and the singles also weren't quite as successful: Both "Trouble" and "God is a DJ" missed the Top Forty entirely, a far cry from the chart domination of her previous album. Still, these singles were far more successful elsewhere. "Trouble" especially connected with fans and became a Top Ten hit in Australia, Ireland, Germany, Sweden, and the UK. (In a nice twist, the UK star Shakin' Stevens had a Top Twenty hit with a 2005 cover of the song.)

"Trouble" also had a Sophie Muller-directed music video that was Pink's most fully realized cinematic statement to date. Set in the rough-and-tumble old west, the clip finds Pink portraying a sassy, take-no-prisoners dame who lays waste to cowboys and bar patrons alike. In a memorable scene, she seduces a jail sheriff (played by actor Jeremy Renner) and handcuffs him to a window so she can escape prison.

The video for "God is a DJ" had a different vibe entirely, but was no less engaging. A sequel of sorts to "Get the Party Started," the clip found Pink and her party-loving club kid friends heading to a night out. Unlike the earlier video, however, she's granted entrance to the club without subterfuge—a nod to the song's optimistic, world-is-my-oyster vibe.

Try This arrived at a time when pop music was also undergoing changes, in no small part because of Pink

KORG

Left: Pink performs onstage at the Point Theatre, Dublin, Ireland, opening the European leg of her *Try This* tour, February 19, 2004

and *M!ssundaztood*. Pop-punk newcomers Avril Lavigne and Fefe Dobson, rock-influenced songwriter Michelle Branch and the new wave-inspired band No Doubt gave mainstream music harder edges. On the horizon was an even harder wave of emo-punk from Fall Out Boy, My Chemical Romance and Paramore; had *Try This* been released a few years later, it might have performed better in America.

Still, the album was much more of a success in Europe. Pink went on a large-scale tour that wound through major cities in Ireland, Germany, Switzerland, France, Austria, and England, as well as Australia and Europe. Footage from a 2004 tour stop in Manchester, England, revealed a high-energy encore that opened with a faithful cover of Guns N' Roses' hard rock classic "Welcome to the Jungle." Pink, wearing a floor-length, orange cape with black stripes and bug-eye sunglasses, greeted fans in the crowd before heading front and center to belt out the song. The show-stopping "Get the Party Started" was even more impressive. Pink lifted herself up onto a pink ribbon that dropped from the ceiling, hanging upside down at one point and ending the song spinning around in the air like a top. The move was a preview of even more impressive acrobatics she'd unleash in the coming years.

Years later, Pink had better perspective on her mindset circa *Try This*. "Professionally, when I went from *M!ssundaztood* to *Try This*, I was sort of like 'I'm gonna rebel, and you think I can't do punk rock,'" she told the *Los Angeles Times*. "I was rebelling for no reason ... had I stayed on my path and not worried so much about what other people said I couldn't do I would have probably been all right. But anything I was gonna do after *M!ssundaztood* was gonna be a failure. After something that big, anything is gonna suck to people."

Opposite: Pink, Britney Spears, and Beyoncé Knowles pose on the steps of the National Gallery in London, on January 26, 2004, for the launch of Pepsi's new TV commercial

Below: Janis Joplin—who Pink was due to portray in biopic, *The Gospel According to Janis*—pictured circa 1970

Although *Try This* wasn't an across-the-board global commercial success, Pink's star was still ascending. She won a Grammy Award for Best Female Rock Vocal Performance for "Trouble" in February 2004. That same year, she teamed up with Beyoncé and Britney Spears in a Roman competition-themed Pepsi commercial, performing Queen's "We Will Rock You" in front of an emperor (played by Enrique Iglesias) and members of Queen. Pink led the charge on the song, screaming the iconic chorus to kick off the song.

Pink also spread her wings writing for other people. She teamed up again with Dionne Warwick's son, musician and producer Damon Elliott (who appeared on *M!ssundaztood* and *Try This*) to pen "Take A Picture," which surfaced on *Moodring*, the album by her "Lady Marmalade" co-singer Mýa. The following year, she also guested on Lisa Marie Presley's midtempo ballad "Shine," from the album *Now What*.

In 2004, news broke that Pink was due to portray one of her idols, the late rocker Janis Joplin, in a biopic called *The Gospel According to Janis*. "I relate to her a lot and I know a lot about her life," she said in an interview. "She was a white girl singing the blues and so was I, and it wasn't widely accepted. I hide my pain, that's why I'm always laughing, and she was kind of like that. She was very funny 'cos she was in a lot of pain."

Unsurprisingly, Pink's screen test for the film was off-the-charts good and authentic. The biopic's intended director, Penelope Spheeris—who was also behind the camera for *Wayne's World* and the legendary punk documentary *The Decline of Western Civilization*—was quoted by *Rolling Stone* as saying Pink's screen test was "the most gratifying moment of my whole career. ... To see this girl bring Janis to life was profound." In fact, Pink won the role with an intense tryout that included

Opposite: Engaged. Pink and Carey Hart at the Cabana Club in Hollywood, California, 2005.

acting in four scenes and singing Joplin songs. "She can sing Janis with her heart and soul without it being pure mimicry," producer Peter Newman added. "It's something very raw and immediate."

At the time, *The Gospel According to Janis* was due in 2005. However, the movie didn't surface that year—and, in 2006, Pink ended up dropping out of the film, citing "scheduling conflicts" as well as some casting issues. Although news reports made it sound as though Pink had secured the lead role, she later claimed that Britney Spears, Lindsay Lohan and Scarlett Johansson were also up to portray Janis. "They're trying to turn it into some circus pop contest—who's the 'it' girl ... who wants to play Janis," Pink said. "Janis was so much deeper than that." Actress Zooey Deschanel was also linked to the movie, but ultimately the production was shelved.

In Pink's personal world, changes were also afoot. She became engaged to Carey Hart in June 2005 and they married in early 2006. By this time, Pink was firmly immersed in preparing her next album, *I'm Not Dead*. Even if *Try This* hadn't lived up to commercial expectations, she picked herself up and moved forward.

"I don't judge myself on how well my songs do at radio, or how much my album sells," she told the *Montreal Gazette* in late 2003. "A failure and a success is all how you look at it. I've been creative to my highest potential at this point of my life, and I'm super-proud of myself for making it this far." Pink added that she was just twenty-four years old and had already accomplished many of her childhood goals. "Now it's just about having fun and causing chaos, and doing [whatever] I want to do."

That mantra wasn't far removed from what Pink had already done—but in the coming years, she would be branching out creatively and speaking her mind even more forcefully.

> **"I've been creative to my highest potential at this point of my life, and I'm super-proud of myself for making it this far. Now it's just about having fun and causing chaos, and doing [whatever] I want to do."**

I'M NOT DEAD

In a 2003 interview with *The Guardian* around the release of *Try This*, Pink discussed her long-time struggles with physical perfection—or, in her case, dealing with the fact that growing up as a gymnast, her body was "always muscular, always thicker than the average girl." She noted that Marilyn Monroe and other older pin-ups were also like this, and shared that she's come to a place of acceptance with her own ever-changing shape. "I've accepted it now, that I have the ability to gain weight and to lose it. That's why girls can relate to me, because I am not trying to be something else. And if that is empowering to a girl at a difficult time in her life, when body image is all—well, that's awesome."

This topic was still on Pink's mind while writing her fourth album, *I'm Not Dead*. Musically, the full-length refined and elevated the rock-pop sound she favored, with the occasional meditative moments, like the chiming ballad "I Got Money Now" and the Bon Jovi-esque acoustic rocker "The One That Got Away." The latter especially stood out for its delicious details: Pink describes being in the kitchen with the slipped-through-her-fingers guy as he makes cappuccino, sending both into fits of laughter—because, after all, who makes cappuccino?

She introduced her new era to the world with a blunt single and video called "Stupid Girls." The song brazenly courted controversy: It was a no-holds-barred condemnation of society's obsession with physical perfection and celebrities who get ahead by focusing on fashion over brains. Lyrics reference tiny dogs and skimpy shirts, trips to Fred Segal and push-up bras—very pointed references to many of the paparazzi faves at the time—and criticize women for sacrificing their dreams in favor of fame. One memorable line mentions someone dancing in a 50 Cent video after having ditched their ambition of being president.

Whereas Pink's previous hit, "Don't Let Me Get Me," expressed her anxiety around idolized female celebrity and how it made her feel that she didn't measure up, the "Stupid Girls" slams were meant as insults—and she was using these critiques to make a point about the dangers of elevating unrealistic body image portrayals. "An awful lot of people are relieved that someone's actually talking about these things in public," she told the *Irish Times*. "What has surprised me most is that a lot of people agree with the point but hate that it's coming from me. I've been called a hypocrite. Then again, I've also been called fat. Some people have been offended by it, but that's cool, I like to push those buttons. I like dissent in the ranks."

The "Stupid Girls" music video was also polarizing. It was "the most fun video I have ever made in my life," she told the website Generation Q, despite the fact she chipped a bone in her wrist and left the shoot with bruised legs from filming a scene with football players. Her seventh collaboration with Dave Meyers, the clip starts with the premise that Pink is both an angel and devil on the shoulder of a young girl being exposed to mixed messages about her future. This gave Pink the chance to portray a variety of different characters: a no-nonsense politician, a prim instructor teaching etiquette, a girl on a bowling date comparing herself to a busty lane-mate, and various debutantes. These portrayals can be exaggerated—one scene finds Pink trying to look sexy washing a car and instead coming off as ridiculous—or unflattering: One socialite doesn't know how to drive and keeps hitting people, while another gets an overly orange spray tan.

Previous: Pink opens for Justin Timberlake on his FutureSex/LoveShow 2007 world tour, iPay One Center, San Diego, January 8, 2007

Opposite: Performing "Stupid Girls" during Nickelodeon's 19th Annual Kids' Choice Awards show, April 1, 2006

Stupid Girls

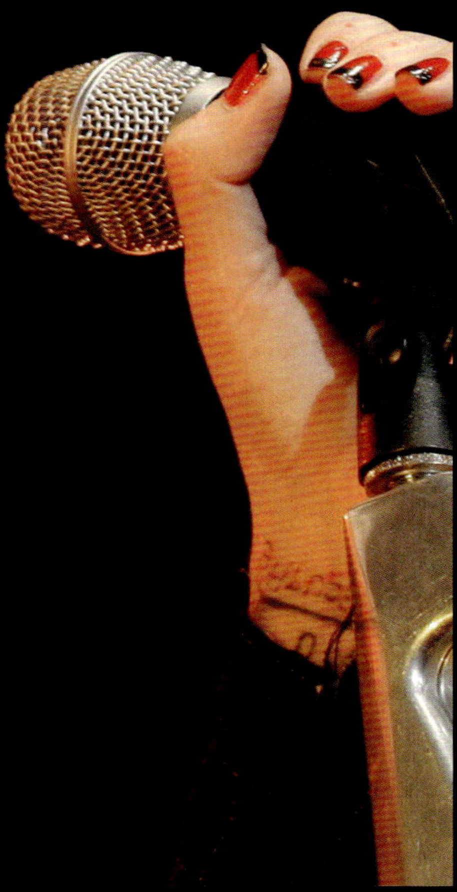

"I've accepted it now, that I have the ability to gain weight and to lose it. That's why girls can relate to me, because I am not trying to be something else. And if that is empowering to a girl at a difficult time in her life, when body image is all—well, that's awesome."

Above: Pink during her concert at the Vtm TV Studio, Belgium, May 18, 2006

Opposite: Pink wins Best Pop Video Award for "Stupid Girls," presented by Nick Lachey (center) and Nicole Richie (right) at 2006's MTV Video Music Awards

These depictions reflected Pink's frustrations with many of the other women earning attention at the time. "These girls have dumbed themselves down to appear cute. How bad is that?" she told the *Irish Times*. "And the way it is now, I feel that it's just the one image of women out there which is being fed to society. There need to be more alternatives, options and examples about how you can be cool without the silly handbag and without acting like a bimbo."

Naturally, all of this didn't go over well with some of the women obviously being spoofed in the video, such as heiress Paris Hilton. "I didn't hear from any of these girls directly, but I got some calls from certain publicists," Pink told the *Irish Times*. "They wanted an advance copy of the song." (She declined.) However, the "Stupid Girls" video does have some serious messages. Pink is pictured looking terrified on an operating table getting prepped for extensive plastic surgery, while a separate scene shows her and another woman in the bathroom purging their meager meals.

In response, the International Association of Eating Disorder Professionals released a statement noting the song "highlights the culture's relentless and unrealistic pursuit of thinness and unattainable drive for physical beauty." While declining to "endorse Pink's personal position," the statement added, "but at the same time we applaud a recording artist who states that if women waste their time, money and energy on trying to be someone else's idea of 'fabulous', they waste their potential to be something better."

Pink told the *Irish Times* this statement was particularly meaningful to her. "These diseases—and they are diseases—are very, very unhealthy. The video started off being humorous, but the point is there that you don't have to kill yourself to meet society's ideal for beauty." It's difficult to quibble with this sentiment—and, in the modern world where social media espouses unrealistic beauty expectations, it's still relevant.

However, in other respects the "Stupid Girls" lyrics and video haven't aged well. For starters, any pop star today who shamed other women (or called them names) would receive blowback for these comments. In a 2021 piece for Pajiba with a striking headline ("STUPID GIRLS" STANDS AS A MISGUIDED FEMINIST CALL IN THE AGE OF BUBBLEGUM MISOGYNY) writer Kayleigh Donaldson also noted how "staggeringly nasty" the video is. "It's not just that Pink is lambasting these bad faith narratives about good girls versus bad ones with no sliver of acknowledgment for how effing hard it is to survive under patriarchy; it's that she gets hyper-specific in her targets."

Despite its controversy, "Stupid Girls" launched Pink's comeback. On January 30, 2006, the video premiered on MTV's *TRL* and debuted on the countdown on January 31, entering at No. 10. The "Stupid Girls" video would go on to peak at No. 6 on the show. Chart-wise, the single immediately performed better in the US than any other song from her previous album, 2003's *Try This*, peaking at No. 13 on the *Billboard* Hot 100; it also reached the Top Ten in countries around the world. Pink received the MTV Video Music Award for Best Pop Video and earned a nomination for the Grammy Award for Best Female Pop Vocal Performance.

"Stupid Girls" was far from the only bold statement on *I'm Not Dead*. Anyone who thought Pink might have been chastened by the commercial performance of *Try This*, was sorely mistaken. If anything, being perceived as an underdog made her double down on refusing to sugarcoat her opinions or thoughts. (Among other

things, the title *I'm Not Dead* could also be seen as pointed self-deprecation, especially since it came after an album that many considered to be a slump.) And in true Pink fashion, she touched on deeply painful experiences. For example, the driving pop-rock song "Long Way to Happy" is based on a poem she wrote at age thirteen that deals with sexual abuse. "I know a lot of people that have been abused and/or molested and/or fucked over by someone close to them," she told *The Independent*, "and I'm no exception. And that's that song." The piano-sparkled orchestral ballad "Conversations With my 13 Year Old Self" is also moving, a compassionate hug across generations to her younger, troubled self.

"I didn't expect to be so emotionally involved in this album," she said in 2007. "I guess I was just kind of at that place where I felt like I had something to add to the world, I feel like there's a hole and I know how to fill it, people aren't talking trash anymore. I was just feeling really creative and emotionally available again."

Other places on *I'm Not Dead* push topical boundaries or confront taboos. Take the pulsating bonus track "Fingers," a song about masturbation, and the guitar-heavy pop song "U + Ur Hand," named after a crude phrase for the same act.

This personal, strong songwriting ensured a warm reception for *I'm Not Dead*. Released on April 4, 2006, the album debuted at No. 6 on the *Billboard* Top 200, selling 126,000 copies its first week on sale, and topped the charts in Australia, Germany, New Zealand, and Switzerland. In spite of this strong start, *I'm Not Dead* couldn't maintain this momentum in the US. In fact, the full-length dropped off the *Billboard* album charts by September and didn't return until early 2007. It

Opposite: Music producer Butch Walker (right) pictured with Avril Lavigne and her then husband Deryck Whibley in 2006

Below: Producers Max Martin (right) and Dr. Luke Gottwald (left) pictured in 2011 at the ASCAP Pop Music Awards

looked like the commercial underperformance of *Try This* might happen again in America.

However, "U + Ur Hand," which had been a hit outside of America but not released as a US single until fall 2006, redeemed *I'm Not Dead*. Pink tells off lame guys who attempt to pick her up while she's enjoying herself at a bar. She stresses that her actions aren't for them—or meant to titillate them—and she's in no mood to answer a booty call. The video is just as striking. Pink dons a variety of costumes to represent different sides of a badass woman—tough car mechanic, buff gym rat, club kid with cherry-red hair and a matching leotard, glamorous gothic vixen—who act out the song's lyrics.

"U + Ur Hand" became a huge hit for Pink: It was her first single to be certified platinum in the US and peaked at No. 9 on the *Billboard* Hot 100, while also topping the Mainstream Top Forty chart. This matched the song's success around the world; it also hit the Top Five in multiple places, including Australia, Germany, Sweden, and Switzerland. However, the song's lyrics caused an uproar because they referenced what online tabloid TMZ characterized as "self-love." In other words, Pink repeatedly told the pesky guy his post-club companion would be his hand, not another person. "I've heard the expression a bunch, mostly out of a guy's mouth: 'Oh, looks like it's just me and my hand tonight,'" Pink said in an interview about the making of the video, "and I just thought it was funny. So I wrote a song about it."

Not everybody thought it was amusing. Before a guest performance on *American Idol*, the reality talent show asked Pink to change the song title to "U + Ur Heart" and make the lyrics more G-rated. "Standards and practices at [TV channel] Fox did not approve the song," Pink's publicist said. "We felt there was no way around what the song is about." Indeed, Pink staunchly refused to change the lyrics, and later told an interviewer incredulously she'd said, "You want me to rewrite my song for you. For *American*-f—king *Idol*? I'm like, what does that even mean, how do you have sex with your heart?"

Pink performed the single "Who Knew" on the show in its place. This introspective song was based on a pivotal and heartbreaking moment from Pink's turbulent past: At age fourteen, she discovered a male friend had overdosed on drugs. "Most of the people at the funeral

Above: Pink, Wembley Arena, UK, December 4, 2006

"I turned twenty-five and I just kind of woke up and realized I have so much to learn, whereas before I thought I knew everything."

were just children," she told the *Daily Mail.* "It should have been a wake-up call for me, but it wasn't." She was also into drugs at the time, as "some of my friends were selling crack," she added. Accordingly, the bittersweet lyrics memorialize her friend and express fond memories of his life and their friendship.

Although she had covered similar thematic ground on past albums, including *M!ssundaztood*, "Who Knew" felt deeper and more emotional than her other songs, notably because her smoky vocal performance is richer and more dynamic: restrained when needed, and cracking with emotion on more heart-wrenching lines. The "Who Knew" music video was also more meditative and cinematic. Pink plays a carnival attendee sporting short, blonde curly hair with tips dyed bright pink. In between footage of her singing directly into the camera are scenes of a young couple who represent and act out the song's sorrows.

In the US, "Who Knew" became a major hit after "U + Ur Hand," going platinum while reaching No. 1 on both *Billboard*'s US Adult Top Forty and US Mainstream Top Forty charts. It nearly topped the overall singles chart in Australia, stalling at No. 2, and also fared well in Canada, Ireland, Germany, and the UK. The success of "Who Knew" was also a sign that Pink's career upheaval was showing signs of abating. Part of this shift had to do with the fresh creative injection from new collaborators.

One notable new face was producer and writer Butch Walker, then riding high with his rock-oriented solo music and the success of his work on Avril Lavigne's *Under My Skin.* Walker was no stranger to career ups and downs—before going solo, he had tenures in the hair metal band SouthGang and power-pop act the Marvelous 3—but he brought an ear for airtight hooks and arrangements to his collaborations. He and Pink came up with the crunchy pop-rock song "Leave Me Alone (I'm Lonely)," a lighthearted song all about needing space from your partner—and spending enough time apart to make reuniting that much sweeter after an absence.

Pink also teamed up with Swedish super-producer and writer Max Martin, known for his work with Backstreet Boys, Britney Spears and Kelly Clarkson, and Dr. Luke; the latter was then in the early stages of becoming one of music's most in-demand studio collaborators. Martin and Luke co-wrote and co-produced three songs on *I'm Not Dead,* including "Who Knew" and "U + Ur Hand."

Despite the success of these songs, it appears Dr. Luke's working relationship with Pink wasn't great. Years later, when the pop star Kesha and Dr. Luke were involved in a lawsuit, Pink didn't mince words when talking to the *New York Times* in 2017 about her one-time collaborator. Pink said she "do[es] not work with him," and added, "He doesn't do good business, he's not a kind person, he doesn't do the right thing when given ample opportunities to do so, and I don't really feel that bad for him."

Circa *I'm Not Dead*, Pink paired her usual blunt honesty with open-mindedness—and a newfound sense of the world around her. *I'm Not Dead* "definitely came from the awakening—it felt good to feel again," she told website Generation Q. "I kind of woke up. I turned twenty-five and I just kind of woke up and realized I have so much to learn, whereas before I thought I knew everything. That's definitely a huge part of that title." To *The Independent*, she added: "I started reading the *New York Times*. I started caring less about my drama and more about the world around me."

This awakening came in part from turmoil in her personal life. Although she had celebrated getting married in 2006, her beloved dad had a heart attack around this time. Fittingly, *I'm Not Dead* closes with a quasi-honor for her father: a solemn folk song called "I Have Seen The Rain," which was the first song she ever learned; her dad wrote it decades before, when he was serving in the military. Pink told *The Independent* she sang the song at Vietnam veteran rallies while growing up. "It was awesome," she said of the experience. To make the song even more special, Pink and her dad recorded the tune together in the studio vocal booth.

"Dear Mr. President," meanwhile, marked her first major foray into political music and raised tough questions. "I love the fact that I can write songs like this," she told CBS. "I have the right to speak my opinion. And be heard. And I feel like more people need to do that. And I have a laundry list of questions for the leaders of this country." With guests the Indigo Girls adding vocals on the chorus, the acoustic song referenced struggles Americans faced—trying to get by while working a minimum-wage job, for example, or homelessness—and critiqued the government's stance on gay rights, women's rights, and incarceration.

Most strikingly, she lamented the distance between politicians and constituents, and accused the powers that be of not knowing what it's like to work hard. It was a bold song for a pop star to release, but it was informed by her own life. "I don't hang out with celebrities," she told *The Independent*. "I hang out with real, nine-to-five people. My family are working-class people. I'm very much in tune with what's [going on]. I don't sit holed up inside my mansion with my poodles and think that everything's fine."

"Dear Mr. President" struck a nerve and topped the charts in Austria and Belgium. But it wasn't Pink's

"I don't hang out with celebrities. I hang out with real, nine-to-five people. I don't sit holed up inside my mansion with my poodles and think that everything's fine."

Above: Pink performs live onstage at the Avo Session, Basel, Switzerland, November 3, 2006

Opposite: Pink impresses with her aerial skills, opening for Justin Timberlake's FutureSex/LoveShow 2007 tour

only musical advocacy during this era. Most notably, she appeared on an all-star track called "Sing" on Annie Lennox's *Songs of Mass Destruction*. Lennox wrote the song to draw attention to the ongoing HIV/AIDS crisis and enlisted twenty-two other women—including Madonna, Bonnie Raitt, Céline Dion, Shakira, and Gladys Knight—to help get her message across.

Collaborations like this one were common for Pink in 2006 and 2007. She appeared on the Indigo Girls' album *Despite Our Differences* on the driving, electrified "Rock and Roll Heaven's Gate," and featured on a remix of India Arie's song "I Am Not My Hair" that appeared in the Lifetime movie *Why I Wore Lipstick to My Mastectomy*. And "Outside of You," another song Pink co-wrote, was recorded by actress-turned-pop-star Hilary Duff on her 2007 album *Dignity*.

In 2006, Pink sang the theme song for *NBC Sunday Night Football*. Dubbed "Waiting All Day for Sunday Night," the song borrows the melody and music from Joan Jett's hard rock anthem "I Hate Myself for Loving You" but inserted football-themed lyrics. (In later years, country stars Faith Hill and Carrie Underwood would put their spin on the song.) Pink handled the song with ease, injecting sass into the commercial tune. She also returned to the world of soundtrack work, contributing a psychedelic funk-rock cover of Rufus and Chaka Khan's 1974 hit "Tell Me Something Good" to the penguin-centered animated film *Happy Feet*.

Pink's big comeback wasn't just limited to music. She also co-starred in the 2007 horror movie *Catacombs*, which follows two sisters as they navigate terrifying scenes at a rave in the Catacombs of Paris.

But, of course, Pink didn't stray too far from her roots as a hard-working touring musician. In April 2007, she released a video, *Pink: Live from Wembley Arena*, that captured the excitement of her December 4, 2006, concert in England to support *I'm Not Dead*. "Rock 'n' roll, yoooo!" Pink screamed before a punkish "'Cuz I Can," as she strutted around the stage dressed in all black, as if she was a member of The Clash. Pop anthems "Just Like a Pill" and "Who Knew" were even more epic in the arena setting, while "God is a DJ" transformed into a strutting soul-pop number that showcased Pink and her talented backup vocalists singing multi-part harmonies. At another point, she even covered her beloved 4 Non Blondes' hit "What's Up?," bringing extra oomph to the already-iconic hit. As per usual during this time, the concert ended with a bang-up, eighties-influenced version of "Get the Party Started" interpolated with Eurythmics' "Sweet Dreams" that saw Pink twirling high above the stage on ribbons. The show set the bar high not just for rock shows, but pop concerts as well.

Although Pink had graduated to being a headliner, she was tapped to open for *NSYNC member-turned-solo-star Justin Timberlake on the early 2007 North American leg of his FutureSex/LoveShow Tour. "My first tour was opening for *NSYNC — had the time of my fucking life — and, 10 tours later, I was opening for Justin," she told *Billboard* in 2019. "The day I saw him at rehearsals, I was like, 'Well, I've come a long way!'"

Pink had indeed come a long way. After some career setbacks, *I'm Not Dead* found her clawing her way back up the charts to pop stardom. Her album sales were up, she reached new chart heights in several countries and her singles were once again commercial successes. However, little did she know that, while her music star would continue to rise, her personal life would be a bumpy ride in the coming years. Pink would need to dig deep and rely on her music for support and survival.

FUNHOUSE

Previous: Pink's *Funhouse* tour comes to KeyArena, Seattle, Washington, September 15, 2009

Above: Pink's stunning performance of "Glitter in the Air," at the 52nd Annual Grammy Awards, 2010

Across the decades, the Grammy Awards has been a showcase for many memorable performances. In recent times, one of the most stunning shows of musical talent and physical dexterity is Pink's 2010 performance of "Glitter in the Air." The appearance starts off low-key, with the singer walking along a stage dominated by simple video screens projecting cool, marbled blue light. Pink wears a floor-length white dress that drapes over her head like a nun's habit but is open in front, exposing delicate, criss-crossed ribbons.

As the piano-driven ballad progresses, however, she slowly walks between the audience to a platform and sheds the dress, leaving her wearing just heels and a nude bodysuit with strategically placed shimmer and strips of fabric. Dancers wrapped in purple ribbons help her into a white fabric sling, which promptly moves upward and, suspended mid-air, she starts spinning around; the choreography and movements resemble a giant mobile hanging over the crowd. Pink then dips her body in water, so when she spins around once again the audience below are sprayed with droplets. The song ends with her hanging upside down by her heels, spinning as furiously as a top, before seamlessly maneuvering herself back to an upright position and slowly lowering herself to the stage with pinpoint precision.

The performance was brave for an awards show. It was graceful and understated, even as it pushed boundaries. Although Pink was used to the performance—she presented the song in a similar fashion in concert around this time—she admitted to BANG Showbiz the Grammys experience was slightly more fraught. "When I do it on tour, I don't have lights above me. There were lights above me, so it almost went into a strobe thing, and I actually did get a little turned around. I thought ... I was going to fall on my nude butt. But I worked it out." Reminiscing about the performance in 2019, Pink expressed even more awe

Opposite: With Carey Hart at Louis Vuitton's Fall/Winter, 2006-2007 ready-to-wear collection in Paris, France

that she was able to pull off what she did. "They let me do a song that wasn't a single, that no one ever heard before," she notes. "They let me fly 100 feet in the air, with no harness, with water. It was so much fun."

Flying high with no safety net doubles as a good summary of Pink's personal life in the preceding few years. After marrying long-time boyfriend Carey Hart in 2006, the couple's relationship had deteriorated. In early 2008, the pair decided to separate. That timing meant Pink was unmoored and reeling from heartbreak while writing and recording her fifth studio album, *Funhouse*. "I was on my own and just a little bit wild," she told *Variety*. "I remember I hadn't spoken to Carey for, like, eight months and it was really painful for me."

Unsurprisingly, marital turmoil overshadowed *Funhouse*. In the official bio on her website homepage, Pink called the full-length her "most vulnerable album to date." Quipping that the album's original name was *Heartbreak is a Motherfucker*, she added, "It's like letting down the armor and admitting I'm human. I'm a girl. We all want to be loved and love. That's all we want."

For comfort and continuity, Pink worked with some familiar faces on the record, including Butch Walker and Billy Mann, the latter of whom had become a trusted collaborator since Pink first worked with him on 2003's *Try This*. The two men co-wrote the quirky, new wave-inspired "Bad Influence," one of *Funhouse*'s highlights, in conjunction with the songwriting duo MachoPsycho. Playing off the carnival theme, the song boasted a rapid-fire vocal delivery, theatrical musical backdrop and dizzying keyboard embellishments. Synth-driven eighties music is also an influence on the album's title track, which was co-written by No Doubt bassist Tony Kanal and Jimmy Harry, the latter who also wrote Kelly Clarkson's hit "Low." Kanal had nothing but positive things to say about Pink. "She's a force to be reckoned with," he told *USA Today*. "She'll do one take of a song, then do it again and give you something completely different." Pink and Mann, meanwhile, delved into more vulnerable territory on "Crystal Ball," a folk-influenced acoustic song about embracing uncertainty and turning bad luck into positives.

In the end, multiple songs directly and honestly addressed her volatile relationship with (and consequent split from) Hart. The midtempo, meditative "Please Don't Leave Me" describes the push-pull of a relationship. The protagonist freely admits they can be a jerk, nearly to the point of being abusive, but asks their ex to stay anyway. This song in particular feels plucked from real life; Pink recalled being in Sweden reuniting with producer/songwriter Max Martin on "Please Don't Leave Me," but Hart still wouldn't answer his phone when she called. Despite the trauma at the song's core, Pink sees some humor in it anyway—mainly that despite not always being her best self, she is trying to be a better person and is learning about herself and evolving every day.

Pink and Martin also teamed up to co-write the orchestra-swept ballad "I Don't Believe You," a song on which she dares her ex to say they have moved on and aren't still in love. (Spoiler: She doesn't believe the ex.) In the official homepage bio, Pink described "I Don't Believe You" as "one of my favorite songs because it's just so naked. It's like taking a deep breath and saying, 'Here I am. Take me. Take your best shot.'" Later, in another interview, she recalled being in the studio and listening to this song with "tears running down my face" and having an intense reaction. "[It's] just like 'Fuck, really?' It's the vulnerable weak side of me that

Below: Pink filming the music video for "So What?" on the streets of Beverly Hills, California, August 6, 2008

I don't let out very often . . . I just love it, it's very near and dear to me."

"Mean," which Pink envisioned as the kind of country-leaning song Aerosmith favored in the late eighties and early nineties, is also vulnerable, although bittersweet. She remembers the good times and sweet gestures of a relationship—him holding the door for her, giving flowers, looking at her lovingly—and laments that this kindness has curdled and been replaced by volatility and disagreements.

However, *Funhouse*'s brash, taunting first single, "So What," made an even bigger impact. Pink puts on a brave face about the breakup—she proclaims she's a "rock star" with "rock moves" while singing about going on a bender and getting into trouble—and says she's better off without her ex. In fact, Pink sounds absolutely *delighted* at the thought her ex might hear the song on the radio and get mad. But despite the breezy, self-empowering lyrics, "So What" has an obvious undercurrent of anger, as Pink also mentions that he let her down and wasn't there to support her.

Understandably, the song's lyrical content raised some eyebrows, as it *seemed* like Pink was slamming Hart very publicly. However, she later clarified that wasn't her intention by having Hart appear in the Dave Meyers-directed "So What" video. "At first I was kind of irked because everyone was like, 'Well, wait. I thought the split was amicable and now she's talking shit about him?! What the fuck?' It's hypocritical,'" she said in her bio. "But once everyone saw the video and saw that Carey was in it, it shut everybody up, which was lovely."

Hart is a good sport about the cameo—even when, in a completely meta-move, Pink trolls him by singing the song's lyrics about an unsupportive partner directly to him, as headlines about their split flash behind them. In addition to Hart's appearance, the video takes a tongue-in-cheek look at their breakup—the first scene features her getting a big red tattoo that says VOID over lovey-dovey ink—and her divorce rebellion: She's portrayed pissing off drivers by gleefully (and slowly) riding a lawn mower in traffic, getting naked on a red carpet and cutting down a tree with their initials.

The song clearly hit a nerve: Released in August 2008, "So What" burned up the singles chart, hitting No. 1 on the *Billboard* Hot 100 just four weeks after its release. It was the first Pink single to top the charts in the US since "Lady Marmalade." Additionally, "So What" topped the charts around the world, in Australia, Canada, Germany, New Zealand, and the UK. A raucous performance at the MTV Europe Video Music Awards in early November aided the song's success. Pink starts the performance grabbing a shot from show host Katy Perry and then breaks what looks like an empty wine bottle over the head of a nearby audience member. From there, she cops nothing but attitude as she sings while winding through the crowd, before eventually ending up onstage finishing the song as a massive pillow fight erupts around her.

"Sober," the follow-up to "So What," was another global hit. The explosive pop-rock tune was more serious, as it features a narrator contemplating an existence without substances and musing aloud about how to get to a place where they're experiencing life's highs without chemical enhancement. "Sober" arose from Pink's own experiences being at a party in her own house. "I didn't want to be there, I didn't want anyone else there," she told MTV's Choose or Lose. "And I had this line in my head saying, 'How do I feel this good sober?' It's not just about alcohol; it's about vices. We all have different ones. We try to get away from ourselves and find our 'true selves' and then we do these things that take us so far from the truth." The Jonas Åkerlund-directed music video mirrored this theme, as it featured Pink and a non-sober version of herself attending the same party and interacting with one another. At one point, sober Pink comforts her drunk self as she throws up in the bathroom; at another point, the two Pinks are depicted making out together on a bed.

Right: A raucous performance at the 2008 MTV Europe Music Video Awards in Liverpool, UK

This assessment tracks with how often Pink stressed that *Funhouse* wasn't just about her relationship dissolving or about weighty topics. In fact, other songs touch on hedonism, pleasure and having a good time—sometimes too much fun. Take "One Foot Wrong," which describes being on the brink of darkness due to overindulgence. "I used to be into a lot of crazy shit," she said. "Acid's the most awful drug ever. Don't take it. But that song is also about losing control and how easy it is to lose the plot in life and teeter on the edge."

The idea that your perspective can flip on a switch—that something can be great fun until suddenly it's not—informs *Funhouse*. That the title references something you'd experience at a carnival is no accident. Pink said: "Clowns are supposed to be happy, but they are really scary. Carnivals are supposed to be fun, but really they are kind of creepy. But we go and we buy cotton candy and we force our laughter and we get on rides and we strap ourselves in and we do it."

To her, however, this was a good description of life *and* love. "Love is supposed to be fun, but it can sometimes be really scary," she continued. "And the funhouse mirrors that make you look so distorted that you don't recognize yourself and you ask yourself, 'How did I get here? How do I get out of here?' But you think that you want to do it again."

Released in October 2008, *Funhouse* debuted at No. 2 on the *Billboard* Top 200, selling 180,000 copies its first week in stores. It did even better around the world, topping the charts in Australia, Ireland, New Zealand, Switzerland, and the UK. Pink celebrated the commercial success with a dramatic performance of "Sober" at the following month's American Music Awards, backed by a string section and her electric rock band.

Opposite and right: Pink onstage during her *Funhouse* tour, KeyArena, Seattle, Washington, September 15, 2009

As Pink's commercial fortunes grew, her live performances became more intricate. On the *Funhouse Tour*—which kicked off in Nice, France, on February 24 and ran through much of 2009 across Europe, Australia, and North America—the stage was an ambitious, multi-level construction designed to look like an ornate carnival funhouse, complete with a trampoline-like bed. Concerts started off with her covering AC/DC's "Highway to Hell" offstage before she emerged from underneath the stage in a cloud of smoke and spun on a wire high above the crowd, a red feather plume trailing behind her.

Later in the set, she and a dancer performed "Sober" while suspended in the air over the stage via a trapeze. The premise allowed her to do graceful acrobatic moves that revealed her gymnastic training; in fact, at times the choreography resembled an uneven bars routine. Pink hung upside down with the dancer holding her ankles and even flipped in the air in the process. To make the choreography that much more impressive, she was lifted up to the trapeze while blindfolded. (Months before her legendary Grammys performance, Pink stunned 2009 MTV Video Music Awards viewers by doing a similar routine.)

Pink intuitively understood that a good set required dynamic pacing and that meant breaks from spectacle or chances of injury. The setlist included a cover of Queen's "Bohemian Rhapsody," which gave her (and her band) the chance to show off their hard-rock chops. As the song crested, she even grabbed a drumstick and banged on the drumkit. In sonic contrast, Pink also slotted in an acoustic set that gave her a breather. She chose to indulge her folk-rock side, performing a stripped-down version of her own "Trouble" and a cover of Led Zeppelin's take on "Babe I'm Gonna Leave You." At another point, Pink transformed Divinyls' "I Touch Myself" into a smoldering, seductive slow jam: She writhed on a chaise lounge

P!NK

Left: *Funhouse* comes to Madison Square Garden, New York City, October 5, 2009

while disembodied hands massaged various parts of her body.

During the summer of 2010, she embarked on a stadium tour in the UK and Europe dubbed the Funhouse Summer Carnival Tour. She mixed up the setlist, bringing back her cherished cover of 4 Non Blondes' "What's Up?" and also performing a medley that featured The Who's "My Generation," Green Day's "Basket Case" and the Police's "Roxanne."

Pink is known for being meticulous about her performances—with good reason, since all of these stunts had little margin for error and any slip-ups could be terrifying. During a July 2010 concert in Nuremberg, Germany, the worst-case scenario happened: News sites reported Pink "fell out of a harness which was supposed to carry her across the crowd," meaning she was "dragged into a barricade." Fortunately, she was okay, and even tweeted from the ambulance, "Nothing's broken, no fluid in the lungs, just seriously sore," while apologizing to fans.

Pink's hard work paid off, and the *Funhouse Tour* ended up being a rousing success. Over 2009 and into 2010, the *Funhouse Tour* and the Funhouse Summer Carnival Tour together reportedly sold a staggering three million tickets. There was no rest, however. As this touring wound down, another blockbuster effort was brewing: a hits collection, *Greatest Hits ... So Far!!!*, to celebrate her first decade in the industry. "At the end of the day, when I get out of my own way, which is what I had to do, it's something to really be proud of, because when I was a little girl, all I wanted to do was make one hit record," she told InDemand.fm. "To be able to put out an album full of them is pretty damn special."

In addition to Pink classics, the compilation included a new song, "Raise Your Glass," which was inspired by this heavy round of touring—and

"I want to write a song for my fans around the world. To me it's about being an underdog and celebrating imperfections and celebrating the fact that we're dirty little freaks."

Opposite: Pink performs "Raise Your Glass" at the American Music Awards, in Los Angeles, on November 21, 2010

dedicated to all of her supporters. "I want to write a song for my fans around the world," DigitalSpy quoted her as saying in a promo video. "To me it's about being an underdog and celebrating imperfections and celebrating the fact that we're dirty little freaks." Fittingly, the upbeat song boasts an exuberant tone that's like a spirited toast in a bar, with a pop edge that crescendos into ecstasy by the song's end.

The "Raise Your Glass" music video, meanwhile, celebrates the joys of being different. Pink portrays a variety of personas—Rosie the Riveter, a tough-as-nails skateboarder, an outmatched wrestler—all of whom exude tenacity and strength. At one point, she even depicts a nerdy underdog at a school dance who finds her match with an equally nerdy beau. "Raise Your Glass" became her third US No. 1 hit and also topped the charts in Australia. "I hit the road and pounded the pavement—and became a touring artist," she told MTV. "You don't have to be popular when you're a touring artist. You just have to be good, and this is just a celebration and a thank-you."

"Raise Your Glass" was followed by another blockbuster smash from *Greatest Hits ... So Far!!!*: "Fuckin' Perfect." The song also encourages people to be OK with who they are, flaws and all, even when it's emotionally difficult. "Fuckin' Perfect" came with a striking video featuring an adult experiencing flashbacks to her difficult childhood. Her younger self, portrayed by actress Tina Majorino, is a moody teenager plagued by self-doubt and insecurities. To compensate, Majorino's character leans on self-harm and disordered eating. As with "Raise Your Glass," however, the video ends on a triumphant note. The teen channels her frustration into painting—and, in the present day, her older self passes on words of wisdom to her own daughter. "Fuckin' Perfect" reached No. 2 in the US, Canada and New Zealand, and the Top Ten in multiple other countries.

Around this time, Pink was on such a hot streak that even songs she *didn't* perform flew up the charts. During the *Funhouse* sessions, Pink co-wrote and recorded the song "Whataya Want from Me" with Max Martin and Shellback. Her version didn't end up on her album, although it later surfaced on the German and Australian versions of *Greatest Hits ... So Far!!!*. However, beloved *American Idol* contestant and later Queen singer Adam Lambert released it as a single after becoming the TV show's runner-up. Lambert's version became a worldwide hit, reaching the Top Ten in Australia, Canada, the US (among other places) and topping the charts in Germany.

Pink for one was thrilled by Lambert's success. "He killed this song," she told the *Los Angeles Times*. "That was fun. I always liked this song; I just didn't want it on the record." She added that *Funhouse* was so focused on her issues with husband Carey Hart that she "didn't want to dilute it with my problems with other people."

Pink's rising star earned her spots on high-profile collaborations. Eminem tapped her for the song "Won't Back Down" on his 2010 album *Recovery*. The rapper specifically chose Pink because of her talent. "I felt like she would smash this record, so I gave her a call and she was with it, so we did it," he said in a radio interview. Separately, she was a soloist in a twenty-fifth anniversary remake of the 1985 charity single, "We Are the World," which was recorded in the wake of the devastating Haitian earthquake.

In February 2011, Pink earned another Grammy Award, for Best Pop Collaboration with Vocals, for a cover of John Lennon's "Imagine" that also featured

Right: At the premiere of *Happy Feet Two* in Los Angeles, California, November 13, 2011, with husband, Carey Hart and daughter, Willow Sage Hart. Pink was the voice of Gloria in the movie.

Herbie Hancock, India Arie, Seal, and others. The song appeared on Herbie Hancock's 2010 album, *The Imagine Project*, which also featured another Pink appearance: She covered the quietly hopeful "Don't Give Up" with John Legend, playing the Kate Bush to his Peter Gabriel. And in November, Pink spread her proverbial wings further and lent her voice to the penguin Gloria in the animated movie *Happy Feet Two*. For good measure, she was also responsible for co-writing and performing the movie's theme song, the soaring piano ballad "Bridge of Light."

By this time, Pink had welcomed her first child, Willow Sage Hart, with Carey. Although *Funhouse* revolved around heartbreak, she and Hart had found their way back to each other during the album's press and promotional cycle. Pink later revealed the reconciliation had started with Hart's cameo in the "So What" video. "Carey hadn't heard the song before he did the video," she said. "That's how much he trusts and loves me. He pretty much just rolls his eyes, throws his hands up in the air, and hugs me. He gets it. He gets me." As it turns out, Pink's suspicions that Hart didn't really want to move on were right. "We never really got divorced," she told BANG Showbiz. "We really hate paperwork. Everything is really wonderful. It's full circle."

Pink had navigated through highs and lows and was on top of the world—in some moments, literally—but was enjoying some rare equilibrium. "I was so f–king lonely," she told *Variety* years later of making *Funhouse*. "And I made one of my best records from heartbreak. ... That album was very successful. Maybe a lot of people were going through a divorce at that moment." As she moved into making new music, Pink was finding her footing and moving forward from a place of power.

Pink and Carey Hart

In fall of 2020, Pink took to Instagram and posted a photo in which she's embracing husband Carey Hart. His back is to the camera, exposing the extensive tattoos inked on his arms, but he is clearly nuzzling Pink's neck. Her eyes are closed, but she has a huge, happy grin. Along with the photo, she added a characteristically candid caption.

"He's still my favorite, sweet little dirtball," she wrote. "He and I have been at this a long time, and it is our relentless and stubborn idealism that keeps us together. Marriage is awful, wonderful, comfort and rage. It is boring, terrifying, and a total nail-biter. It is loving another fallible creature while trying to love yourself. It is a lifetime of coming back to the table."

Few sentences better summarize the pair's relationship which has had its rocky moments but is now one of the most enduring celebrity partnerships. Just as Pink is honest about her musical career—she's also frank about the ups and downs of marriage and parenting.

"There are moments where I look at [Hart] and he is the most thoughtful, logical, constant [person] ... he's like a rock," she told *The Guardian* in 2017. "He's a good man. He's a good dad. He's just the kind of dad I thought he'd be and then some." Then, however, she noted that this feeling could flip on a dime. "And then I'll look at him and go: 'I've never liked you. There's nothing I like about you. We have nothing in common. I don't like any of the shit you like. I don't ever wanna see you again.'"

Still, he and Pink share a penchant for bravery and pushing limits. A California native, Hart grew up riding motorcycles, and started competing as a freestyle motocross racer, attempting jaw-dropping (and dangerous) tricks. The couple's initial meeting was auspicious. While competing at the 2001 X Games in Pink's hometown of Philadelphia, Hart attempted to do a backflip while on his bike, but instead lost control and flew off, landing hard on the dirt track. He broke a bunch of bones, including three ribs, his tailbone and his right foot. "I shook his hand and five minutes later he broke 14 bones," Pink once told an interview dryly. "I had a big effect on him."

Still, these injuries didn't dampen Hart's feelings for Pink. "I knew within the first few weeks after meeting her that I wanted to be with her for the rest of my life," he later told *People*.

The couple started dating, with Hart appearing in the 2002 video for "Just Like a Pill." As their relationship progressed, aligning their schedules could be difficult, as Pink

Left: Pink and Carey Hart, 2009

Opposite above: Pink and Carey Hart at the ESPN Action Sports and Music Awards, 2002

was touring (and based in Los Angeles) and Hart lived in Las Vegas. In interviews dating from early in their relationship, Pink talked openly about the challenges she faced. "It was easier for me when I wasn't in a relationship," she told *The Face* in 2002. "I didn't have anyone to miss, I could focus completely on what I was doing. I had no real reason to go home."

Later in the same interview, she stressed that the relationship she had with Hart was healthier than her previous romantic entanglements. "He's a good guy. I love him, but not in the way that you possess something? He's one of the few that don't think in a certain mind-frame: the cheating and the I-have-to-have-this and it's all about money and looks and ten girls at once and all that dumb stuff."

Their relationship wasn't perfect—in fact, they broke up for about a year in 2003—but they traveled to see each other often and made their partnership work. Unsurprisingly, Pink and Carey Hart's engagement was also wholly untraditional. On June 26, 2005, Hart had an important motocross race, the Pro 250 class finals in Mammoth, California. Pink was there to cheer him on—and pop the question. ("He was never going to ask me because I said 'No' so many times," she said in 2012.) During the race, she held up a sign near the track that said, "Will U marry me?" Focused on the competition, Hart didn't notice the sign or stop.

However, Pink persisted, telling him before the next race he needed to look at the sign she was holding up when he passed. This time, he saw her message—for good measure, she also added the word "Serious!" after her question—and promptly veered off track. According to Pink he responded, "Are you kidding me?" and then quickly said, "Yes."

The pair wasted no time, tying the knot on January 7, 2006, in Costa Rica, on the beach at a Four Seasons resort. According to *People*, the non-denominational sunset ceremony had more than a hundred guests, including Lisa Marie Presley. Pink walked down the aisle to one of her favorite songs, Billy Joel's "She's Only a Woman."

"We wanted it very fun and non-traditional," Hart told *People*. "We're spiritual, but we're not religious. It was about

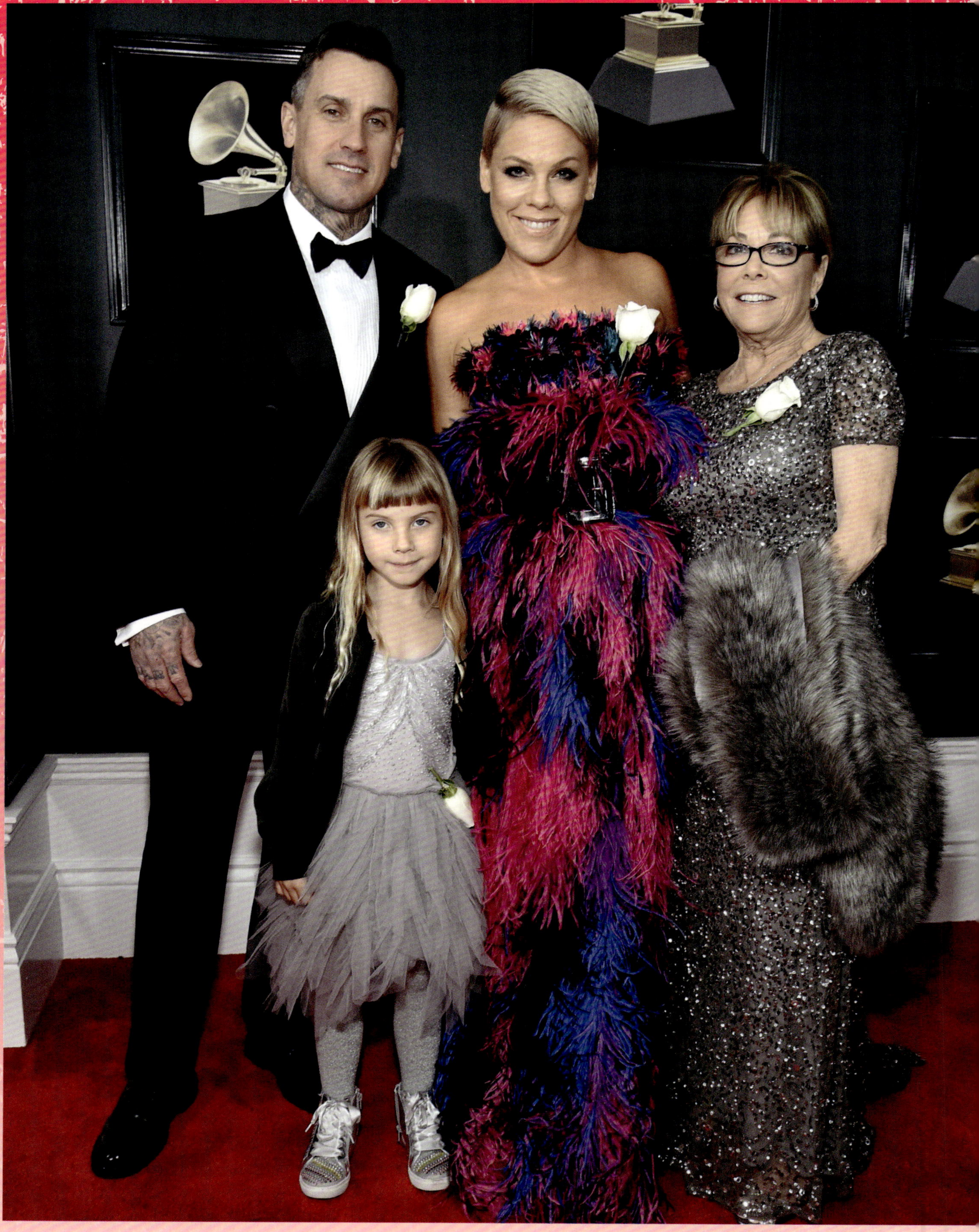

"I knew within the first few weeks after meeting her that I wanted to be with her for the rest of my life."

CAREY HART

being with our closest friends and family and having a very fun and loose party."

The honeymoon period lasted a few years. In February 2008, the couple announced they had separated. "This decision was made by best friends with a huge amount of love and respect for one another," Pink's publicist said. "While the marriage is over, their friendship has never been stronger." Pink herself reiterated that she and Hart remained friends, writing on her website, "The most important thing for you all to know is that Carey and I love each other so, so much. This breakup is not about cheating, anger, or fighting."

What prompted the split, she revealed years later in an interview with *Redbook* magazine, was the same thing they had to navigate early in their dating relationship: busy schedules that made seeing each other difficult. "Carey would see me for five days and be gone for six weeks," Pink said. "We'd try to fix everything in those five days; you just can't do that. And it builds and builds and you don't even know what to say or fight about anymore, and there's no middle ground."

As was her way, Pink channeled her heartbreak into music. Her 2008 album *Funhouse* contained multiple songs about the split, including the massive hit "So What." In a unique twist, Hart actually appeared in the music video for the latter song, which ended up helping thaw the frostiness between them (an effect that hadn't been guaranteed: Pink didn't tell Hart "So What" was about him before he showed up). In the video, she sings about losing her husband as someone holds their hands over her eyes, preventing her from seeing. Lo and behold, the prankster was Hart.

Opposite: Pink and family at the 60th Annual Grammy Awards, Madison Square Garden, New York City, January 28, 2018. (L-R): Carey Hart, Willow Sage Hart, Pink, Judith Moore.

In the end, after eleven months apart, the couple took steps to rekindle their romance. Hart invited Pink to perform on New Year's Eve at his Las Vegas club. She was willing—and brought with her a photo album she had labored over for months that featured mementos from their relationship: cards, snapshots, the works. After soundcheck, Pink gave him the gift.

"On the last page, I pasted a photo of me from a really bad movie I made years ago with my neck slit and blood everywhere," she told *Redbook*. "Next to it I wrote, 'This is me without you.' On the next page, there was a picture of a baby. And I wrote: 'The rest is unwritten.' The divorce papers that we never signed were behind that page. I was like, 'The rest is up to you.'"

Hart very quickly expressed an interest in getting back together, and the couple reconciled. "We crashed a couple of times," Pink told *USA Today*. "Without me wanting to totally admit it. I believe in the work, in the history and in not bouncing from situation to situation. It felt like we weren't finished."

In the subsequent years, Pink and Hart had two children. Daughter Willow Sage arrived first, in June 2011, followed in December 2016 by son Jameson Moon Hart. The expanded family went on the road together when Pink toured. "Going on tour with children is really tricky. It's exhausting. It's the hardest thing I've ever done," Pink said in 2018. "But I'm very, very fortunate that I get to bring my kids with me and that I kind of get to integrate them into my [work] life."

Although parenthood certainly keeps Pink and Hart busy, things are much calmer on the relationship front. "When you first get together, you look at that person as your entire world," she told *People*. "One person can't be your entire world. You have to have your own passions, your own friends, your own time to yourself." Pink admitted she "used to be super-needy" but now has mellowed out. "Now we expect less of each other, and that allows us to give each other more somehow."

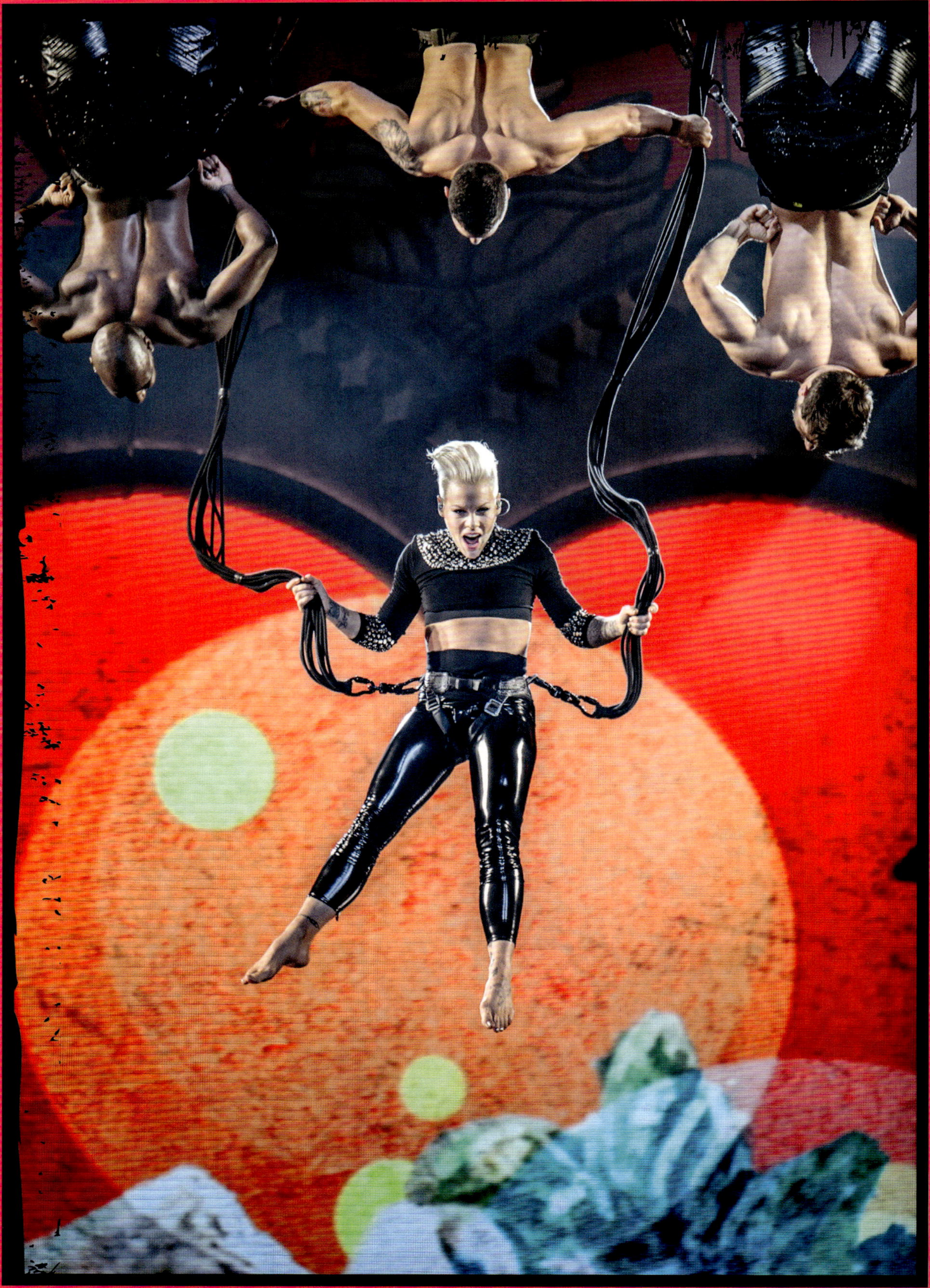

THE TRUTH ABOUT LOVE

Parenthood is one of the biggest things someone can experience. Not only do you have your own physical and emotional changes to contend with, but you're also then tasked with taking care of another person. That can often involve sacrifices, as well as learning how to navigate the heartache, joy, and anxiety that comes with raising kids. It's understandable that new parents might take a step back from their usual routines and get used to their new normal before diving back into their lives.

For Pink, becoming a parent was like an immediate bolt of lightning. The 2011 arrival of her daughter, Willow Sage Hart, brought out her softer side. "I used to be really dark," she told the *New York Daily News*. "Now, I wake up and check her pulse and make sure she's not having a temperature. And then we dance. And we dance, and we dance, and we dance," she says. "Then, we go on bike rides. And we dance some more."

That joy was infectious—but it also served as a creative boost as she started work on her sixth studio album, *The Truth About Love*. In March 2012—a mere nine months after Willow's birth—Pink was already in the studio. "Okay the hair is the palest pink ... You know what that means!!!!!!!!!! NEW RECORD TIME!!!!!!!!!!!!," she tweeted, and noted, "Let's get to making some tuuuunes. Looney tunes."

Pink worked up a staggering forty songs for *The Truth About Love*, she told *Billboard*. "I'm like a faucet—there's nothing going on in my head when I'm off. I write in a journal and that's it. But that first day in the studio just opened up the faucet." Perhaps unsurprisingly, she told *Variety* years later that she was "super-raw at that point in my life," due to new motherhood, which affected the songwriting and recording. "It was the first time that I would work in the studio during the day. I was about to breastfeed and I would put her down for a nap and then come back. It was very kind of daytime-y sober." Keeping the studio hours to weekdays also changed the studio vibe too, she observed. "I felt really present making that record, because normally we'd open a bottle of wine and shit-talk and record at one in the morning. It just wasn't that anymore."

In a blog post on her label's website, she gave hints as to the direction of this new music. "I'm putting my heart and soul into every song and there's a lot of that these days. This little girl has expanded me and what I am capable of feeling as a human. Let's hope it shows." To the *New York Daily News*, she confirmed that her new songs "[reflected] where I am right now" in her life, adding, "I'm just having a lot more fun than I ever have."

Previous: Performing live onstage during the *Truth About Love* tour at United Center, Chicago, November 5, 2013

Opposite: Pink and daughter, Willow, 2009

"I'm like a faucet—there's nothing going on in my head when I'm off. I write in a journal and that's it. But that first day in the studio just opened up the faucet."

Above: Producer and songwriter Greg Kurstin pictured at his home in Los Angeles, on November 14, 2012

Loosening up and having more fun elevated the production and changed her sound. "My goal on this record was to incorporate a little more musicality," Pink told *Rolling Stone*. "Every album, I'm worried that I'm a dork and a fraud – what if I can't sing anymore? Then I stop thinking and start playing guitar, and I realize that it's OK to suck, and move forward. Then it clicks and I'm like, 'I'm fucking awesome!'"

The Truth About Love most definitely didn't suck. In fact, it was Pink's most cohesive album to date, a sleek pop record with a mix of vulnerable ballads, gritty rock nods and kicky retro flourishes. Part of this came with her collaborators, which included familiar names such as Billy Mann and Max Martin and new faces such as producer Greg Kurstin. Kurstin, who worked on four songs with Pink and who had found success for work with Kelly Clarkson and Sia, noticed how quickly and efficiently Pink worked in the studio, particularly with lyrics. "We would finish a song pretty much every day we worked," he told the *New York Daily News*. "She would just do one or two takes, and they were usually amazing. She's just an open book. I think it's why so many different kinds of people relate to her and connect with her."

The Truth About Love proved to be as relatable as previous Pink albums, and illustrated that she hadn't lost any of her edge. Take the punkish "Slut Like You," which relishes sex for the sake of pleasure, or the equally rough-edged "Walk of Shame," a lighthearted look at someone's inner monologue during a morning after a night they somewhat regret. Both are unabashedly honest celebrations of sexuality (and sexual freedom) that put women in the spotlight, a welcome change.

Other songs on *The Truth About Love* delve into deeper emotional territory. Pink told MTV the grimy, Black Keys-esque blues-rocker "How Come You're Not Here" was "like the delusional side of me, where I'm like, 'I'm awesome, why are you not here with me?'" while the string-decorated piano ballad "The Great Escape," which she wrote with Semisonic's Dan Wilson, is "about how I feel the entire world is trying to numb themselves down, whether it be painkillers or anti-depressants." And the

> "She's just an open book. I think it's why so many different kinds of people relate to her and connect with her."
>
> **GREG KURSTIN**

opening track "Are We All We Are" is "my angry protest song," she told *USA Today*. "I'm not broke anymore, but I still have a broke mentality. I have family going through some things. A lot of my friends are single moms or unemployed. It's easy for me to fight their fight."

However, Pink didn't stray too far away from familiar themes, such as the ebb and flow of relationships and the agony such tumult brings. That became obvious with the July 2012 release of *The Truth About Love*'s first single, "Blow Me (One Last Kiss)," a song about finally having enough of a bad situation. "That started with the lyric 'White knuckles and sweaty palms from hanging on too tight.' We're so afraid to lose something —people, jobs, love—that we end up squeezing the life out of it, sabotaging it and losing it anyway." To MTV News, she added, "Well, it's kind of funny with 'Blow Me,' because people are like, 'Oh right, another "F— you" song from Pink. Awesome.' I didn't actually realize that's my theme, but that's been my life, so that's what I write about. But there's also humor; there's a lot of humor and sarcasm always in my lyrics."

That humor surfaces in the winking double meanings to "Blow Me (One Last Kiss)"; the reference to "blow me" in the title refers both to kissing and a more vulgar kiss-off, while the song also references having a "shit day" repeatedly. Pink refused to censor herself despite the profanity: "The record company always says, 'Have you got a clean version?' And I say 'No, just f—ing bleep it. I wasn't going to sing 'You've had a rough day, I've had a rough day,'" she told an Australian website.

The Dave Meyers-directed music video for "Blow Me (One Last Kiss)" illuminated the song's underlying themes. Filmed in black-and-white and scripted like an old-fashioned romance noir movie, the clip finds Pink sabotaging the wedding of an ex. Meyers uses brilliant pops of red to illustrate this heartbreak and revenge: Pink tosses a glass of red wine at the dud dude, while a heart balloon breaks in the air near the end and showers wedding guests with droplets of red, blood-like liquid.

The heartbroken vibe of "Blow Me (One Last Kiss)" resonated with fans. The single peaked at No. 5 on the *Billboard* Hot 100, and also hit No. 1 on both the Dance Club Songs and Mainstream Top Forty charts, as well as topping the Australian singles charts and several Canadian specialty charts.

Below: Songwriter and musician Dan Wilson, 2012

Opposite: Pink and dancer Colt Prattes recreate the music video for "Try" at the 40th American Music Awards, Nokia Theatre, Los Angeles, California, November 18, 2012

The Truth About Love's next single, the Cyndi Lauper-esque, eighties-ballad throwback "Try," also combined striking visuals in the video with meditative lyrics about an imperfect relationship. The song was co-written by the late musician Busbee and Ben West; in fact, the pair recorded the song first when they were in the band GoNorthToGoSouth together. When Pink took a crack at the song, Busbee noted she nailed the song's aching vocal on the first take. "She didn't write that song, but she so felt it and embodied it and took the time to make it her own before she even got there to sing it," he told the And the Writer Is...podcast, adding, "It was as though she wrote it and sang her ass off."

Directed by Floria Sigismondi, the "Try" music video embodies the song's message. Pink and the buff actor Colt Prattes act out a volatile relationship through intricate, physical choreography said to be influenced by the French "Apache Dance." Alternating between loving and tumultuous, the pair's moves are graceful but can be hard to watch because they hint at such interpersonal discord; Pink, who sports a diaphanous dark turquoise outfit and fluorescent hair dye and body-paint, at times resembles an elfin sprite being tossed around carelessly. She recreated the video at the 2012 American Music Awards, in a performance widely considered one of her best awards show appearances.

Although Pink is known for her stubborn individualism, *The Truth About Love* marked her first major foray into high-profile duets. After she appeared on Eminem's 2010 album *Recovery*, he returned the favor and made a cameo on the stomping "Here Comes the Weekend." The negotiation for these appearances was easy, she told *NME*: "He said, 'Do you want to do a song with me?' 'Fuck yeah!' I said, 'Do you want to do a song with me?' and he said, 'Fuck yeah!' Handshake.

SPA

Previous: Nate Ruess (right) joins Pink live onstage during her *Truth About Love* tour, to perform "Just Give Me a Reason," Hamburg, Germany, May 1, 2013

Below: Pink gets up close to fans at Air Canada Centre in Toronto, on November 30, 2013, as a part of her *Truth About Love* tour

Opposite: Pink launches her *Truth About Love* tour, US Airways Center Phoenix, Arizona, February 13, 2013

Nothing signed. Done." She and the UK pop star Lily Allen also teamed up for "True Love," a deceptively sunshine-drenched tune with a soul-pop vibe that spoke to the idea that love isn't all sweet gestures.

However, *The Truth About Love*'s biggest and most successful duet, the midtempo "Just Give Me a Reason" with fun.'s Nate Ruess, almost didn't happen. "He was like, 'I'll just do the demo, 'cause I don't know about duets,' and I totally tricked him into doing it," Pink told Spotify. "I am so glad I was able to. I think now he's very happy that he did it. I think it's a beautiful song and I'm really, really proud of it."

Indeed, Pink had a very clear, defined vision for "Just Give Me a Reason." As the song was coming together, she realized it worked better structured like a conversation between two people in a relationship. "It needs the other perspective, whether it's a guy and a girl, or two girls or two guys," she told Spotify. To explain what she meant, she gave a hypothetical scenario where an innocuous mention of butter spiraled into something completely blown out of proportion.

"I find that there's always one person in the relationship that's feeling a lot more than the other person," Pink said. "I feel like sometimes I'm like, 'The way you passed me the butter this morning, I kinda feel like we're going to be over in a month and we need to talk,' and he's like, 'I just passed you the f—king butter, what are you talking about?'"

"Writing ['Just Give Me a Reason'] was really fueled by the fact that Alecia [Pink] is so strong and independent and so very much herself. At the end of the day, it's so hard to argue against her because what she does is always so great."

NATE RUESS

In practice, "Just Give Me a Reason" is the story about how easy it is to drift apart in a relationship. The initial verses hint at disconnection: Pink starts off by expressing concerns that her partner may be harboring hidden relationship doubts. Ruess chimes in and tries to quell these thoughts with reassurances, although Pink still isn't convinced. In the end, the truth is somewhere in the middle: Without conceding any major rifts, the pair agree that any problems can be fixed and their relationship isn't doomed; it just needs a little TLC.

As the song progresses, Pink and Ruess embody the eventual unity by singing together; their blended voices are full of yearning and longing. Ruess later told MTV that, although his background and experience was markedly different from Pink's musical world—he cut his teeth in an emo-pop band called The Format that were popular in indie-rock circles before forming fun.—he admired Pink's strong-willed vision. "Writing the song was a whole different learning experience and was really fueled by the fact that Alecia [Pink] is so strong and independent and so very much herself. At the end of the day, it's so hard to argue against her because what she does is always so great."

The gorgeous and moving music video helped the song's cause. The main setting is a bare mattress floating on top of clouds, as if to represent the dream mentioned in the lyrics. Pink tosses and turns, as she imagines better days with her tattooed partner (played by her real-life husband) while lamenting the loneliness of their current state. The video is rich with symbolism. At another point, she appears in a pool, stuck under the water, as if she's feeling trapped in her situation. However, she surfaces for air by the video's end, a clear nod to rebirth and rejuvenation.

Ruess also appears in the video, beamed onto a TV like an omniscient presence, sharing his side of things. He and Pink look like they're performing a 1940s-style duet; he is dapper, she sports a frilly dress and a sweeping updo with ringed curls. The video won Best Collaboration at the 2013 MTV Video Music Awards, while the song itself was a monster global hit that shot to No. 1 all over the world, including the US, Australia, Canada, Germany, New Zealand, and Italy. Fittingly, *The Truth About Love* also became Pink's first No. 1 album in the US, selling 280,000 copies during its first week in stores, and topped the charts in Australia, New Zealand, Germany, Sweden, Canada, Austria, and Switzerland. In Australia, *The Truth About Love* topped the ARIA End of Year Albums Chart in 2012 and 2013.

In February 2013, Pink launched *The Truth About Love Tour* in Phoenix, Arizona. It was an immediate hit: In June, *Billboard* reported that she was atop their Hot Tours chart, having grossed $28.3 million for

Opposite: Wowing fans with her jaw-dropping performance during her *Truth About Love* tour

Opposite: Pink delivers a dazzling rendition of "Raise Your Glass" whilst suspended from the ceiling by bungee cords, US Airways Center, Phoenix, Arizona, February 13, 2013

shows in US and Canadian arenas. The very next week, she remained at No. 1 on the chart because receipts had come in from her European tour: Her shows had grossed $30.7 million. As per usual, *The Truth About Love Tour* was an impressive spectacle of vocal talent and jaw-dropping physicality.

During "Raise Your Glass," she hung from bungee cords and did somersaults in the air while singing. Then came "Sober." She started the song inside an egg-shaped contraption that was suspended from the ceiling, and then promptly climbed outside it, clinging to the side with confident ease, as it spun around wildly and rose above the stage. "Try" was also especially epic. At a London show she rose above the stage, pirouetting like a ballerina, before unleashing some truly impressive moves. At one point, she wrapped ropes around her legs and executed a perfect splits in the air, while remaining so evenly balanced that she was able to take her hands off other supporting ropes. A few seconds later, she wrapped the same ropes around her feet and maneuvered her body so she was upside down like a bat. As the song crested, she continued doing what looked like a graceful floor routine, only in the air.

As with other tours, Pink also played covers. Her setlist this time around included a faithful take on Chris Isaak's "Wicked Game" that illuminated her full-throated wail, while Australian shows featured her doing a delicate acoustic version of Cyndi Lauper's "Time After Time."

As if Pink wasn't busy enough touring, winning awards and raising an infant, she also found time for several collaborations. She contributed a soaring vocal hook on "Guns and Roses," from rapper T.I.'s 2012 album *Trouble Man: Heavy Is the Head*, and co-wrote two songs on Cher's 2013 effort *Closer to the Truth*: "I Walk Alone"—to which she also added backing vocals—and the heartfelt "Lie to Me."

That same year, Pink dusted off her acting chops and branched out to appear in the movie *Thanks for Sharing*, which co-starred Mark Ruffalo and Gwyneth Paltrow. The musician portrayed a rough-around-the-edges, unpredictable woman named Dede who lives with a sex addiction. Pink's performance drew favorable praise from rogerebert.com critic Dan Callahan, who wrote, "Of all the cast here, the least experienced is the pop singer Pink, yet she does the best acting in the film: natural, a little harsh, a little unstable."

In a nod to Pink's blockbuster 2013, *Billboard* named her their Woman of the Year. The magazine also reported that *The Truth About Love Tour* was one of the top-grossing tours of 2013, with $147.9 million in ticket sales. The only artists in front of her? Pink's beloved Bon Jovi, along with Cirque Du Soleil's *Michael Jackson: The Immortal World Tour*.

Pink's good fortune continued into 2014, as "Just Give Me a Reason" was nominated for Song of the Year and Best Pop Duo/Group Performance at the Grammy Awards. (Unfortunately, the pair lost to Lorde's "Royals" in the former category and Daft Punk's "Get Lucky" in the latter.) She and Ruess did perform together at the ceremony, bringing her vision of a spirited conversation to life: Both of them became increasingly animated as the song progressed, Ruess especially, as they sang on a catwalk in front of the stage. For good measure, Pink also performed "Try" on the show. She didn't try to top the stunning 2010 Grammys performance of "Glitter in the Air," although she thrilled the audience with a graceful performance that mirrored her tour approach, of singing while suspended in the air by wires and ribbons.

In late April 2014, Pink performed Billy Joel's "She's Always a Woman" with her idol during a radio special. She reiterated how much Joel's music meant to her and her father before singing a lovely, meditative version of the song that was full of restraint and vibrato. Prior to the performance, Joel also discussed the meaning of the song, which he wrote about a woman finding her way in the notoriously sexist music business and dealing with blowback and name-calling. "That was the point of the song," he explained. "They're bitching about her and I'm saying, 'You can bitch all you want, she's great at business and she comes home and she's a woman with me.'"

In hindsight, it's easy to see why Pink gravitated toward that song, beyond the fact it's by Billy Joel: Its underlying message speaks to Pink's own career as a strong woman carving out her own path in the music industry. In a characteristically frank 2012 interview with *USA Today*, she said, "An ambitious man is admirable and respected. An ambitious woman is difficult and emotional. There's a boys' club, even in music. You have to think before you talk. I can be loud, but I've learned you can have quiet power." After *The Truth About Love*, it was clear Pink excelled at pairing her quiet power with a loud, galvanizing roar.

Previous: Pink (credited as Alecia Moore) with Josh Gad in 2012 American comedy-drama, *Thanks for Sharing*, which also co-starred Mark Ruffalo and Gwyneth Paltrow

Above and opposite: Pink performs onstage during the 56th Grammy Awards, Staples Center, Los Angeles, California, January 26, 2014

Right: Performing live onstage with childhood idol Billy Joel in 2014

"An ambitious man is admirable and respected. An ambitious woman is difficult and emotional. There's a boys' club, even in music. I can be loud, but I've learned you can have quiet power."

YOU+ME

Highly creative people always need multiple outlets for their ideas. That's why you often see musicians working as visual artists (or vice versa). Pink certainly qualifies as one of these highly creative people. When she's not working on her own music, she's co-writing songs for other artists, hopping on collaborations or branching out into acting and advocacy.

Throughout the course of building a career, she found a kindred spirit in the Canadian musician Dallas Green. No stranger to musical shapeshifting himself, he cut his teeth in one of Canada's most beloved punk bands, Alexisonfire, before pivoting and exploring his quieter, folk-leaning side with the project City and Colour. Together, Green and Pink formed the musical duo You+Me, and released an album called *rose ave.* in 2014.

Green and Pink first crossed paths in January 2010, when City and Colour was touring the United States. "We played a show in Los Angeles, and she came to it, because she had recently been turned onto my songs," he told the website Alter the Press. "I guess she was really taken to them, which is nice." That meeting went so well that Pink offered City and Colour the chance to open for her in the UK, playing some of the Funhouse Summer Carnival Tour stadium dates.

Green jumped at the opportunity—and wasn't disappointed when he finally caught her in concert, calling her show, "the craziest thing I've ever seen," and praising the fact she still sings live during the elaborate performances. He admitted that Pink's fans weren't necessarily as enthusiastic, perhaps because they weren't familiar with Green or his music, although he told Alter the Press they were at least "polite" during the five-song opening set. He took the reception in his stride, however. "If someone asks you if you want to play for 30,000 people, you say, 'Yes, I would.' It doesn't matter who it is, because chances are, you will get a couple of them coming away thinking, that was good."

Luckily, among those impressed was Pink. "He has the most angelic voice I've ever heard in my life," she said in a promo video announcing You+Me "and I thought, 'Huh. Maybe one day if I get good enough, he'd sing with me.' So I asked him." Both musicians were quite busy, but after Pink wrapped up her *The Truth About Love* obligations, she and Green finally carved out some time to see what magic they could make together.

Pink booked the pair a studio in Los Angeles, and Green came prepared with melodies, guitar parts and voice notes on his iPhone. Although he thought they were just getting together for a songwriting session, the work progressed quicker than either of them anticipated, and they produced a song or two each day. After spending a short time together, they ended up with a record.

The first song that emerged was "From a Closet in Norway (Oslo Blues)," a song about being unsettled and uncomfortable. Their voices rise and fall in tandem, atop sparse and feathery, plucked guitars. Despite the heavy subject matter, "From a Closet in Norway (Oslo Blues)" sounds fluid and airy, like the pair had been recording together for years. Speaking to *Time*, Pink added that she "[didn't] want to say [making the

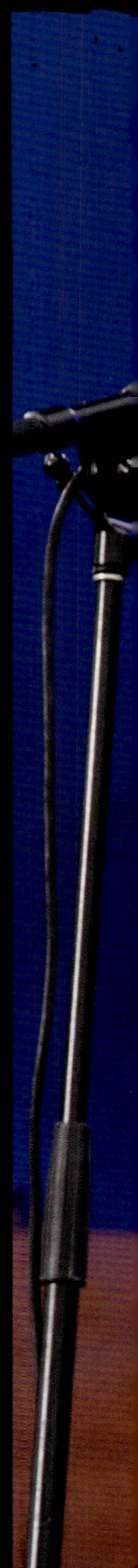

Previous: Folk music duo You+Me, Alecia Moore (Pink) and Dallas Green, 2014

Opposite: Dallas Green, 2014

BMI
BMI
BMI

record] was effortless, but in a way, it was. It was meant to happen. This album is very special to me."

The rest of *rose ave.*—the title refers to the studio's address—is in the same vein as "From a Closet in Norway (Oslo Blues)." The pair crafted spare songs, driven by rich, acoustic guitar, expressive vocals and the occasional overdubbed instrumental flourishes. Yearning pedal steel curls through "Open Door," while solemn organ drones on "Unbeliever." Other songs incorporate piano and percussion, but only enough to enhance what's already there.

The creative process for the album's lyrics reflected a coming-together of different songwriting approaches. "I'm terrified of writing down the wrong thing," Green told *ET Canada*. In contrast, he observed that Pink "writes until she finds the right thing. It was amazing to watch that happen." Thematically, *rose ave.* matches the music's intimate vibe, with songs that ruminate on challenging or frustrating times in the present day. However, there's a streak of optimism throughout: These songs also dream of finding a way toward a better future, even if the current path seems murky.

In the *Time* interview, Green also marveled at how well their voices meshed. "I love that two such giant voices—if I can say so for myself and Alecia—can make an entire record and never once overpower each other. It's astonishing to me how we were able to meld our voices together. It ripped my face off every time we went into the vocal booth." He's not wrong: The pair sound perfect together, with Green's conspiratorial vocal tone and Pink's huskier voice melding into hypnotic harmonies. Although each have their moments of power—Green boasts a dynamic falsetto that cuts glass, for instance—they also intuitively know how to work together for the greater good of a song. On the closer, the piano-only version of Sade's 1992 hit "No Ordinary Love," both musicians turn in restrained vocal performances, transforming the song into an aching, romantic plea.

For Pink, making *rose ave.* was a throwback to a childhood spent listening to songwriting-driven folk music with her dad—acts like Creedence Clearwater Revival, Don McLean, and Simon and Garfunkel. "[My dad and I] used to harmonize really, really well together," she told the *Los Angeles Times*. "I haven't harmonized with someone since my dad like I do with Dallas." However, You+Me was also a way for her to fulfill a long-held wish to sing like a modern folk act; her beloved Indigo Girls. "I grew up listening [to] harmonies, so it was just so yummy to sit on a chair with my

Opposite: Pink and Dallas Green pictured at the 63rd Annual BMI Pop Awards, Beverly Wilshire Hotel, Beverly Hills, California, May 12, 2015

"He has the most angelic voice I've ever heard in my life, and I thought, 'Huh. Maybe one day if I get good enough, he'd sing with me.' So I asked him."

> "I love that two such giant voices—if I can say so for myself and Alecia—can make an entire record and never once overpower each other."
>
> DALLAS GREEN

Previous: Alecia Moore (Pink) and Dallas Green as folk act, You + Me, October 16, 2014

For Pink, making *rose ave.* was a throwback to a childhood spent singing along with her dad to folk music acts such as Creedence Clearwater Revival (below), the Indigo Girls (opposite, top), and Simon and Garfunkel (opposite, bottom)

friend and sing these beautiful harmonies," she told *Time*. "I literally had a smile on my face the entire time."

With *rose ave.*, each artist also had the chance to tap into more primal emotions. For example, Pink decided she wanted to write a song about her mom. It was no secret that she and her mom had an up-and-down relationship over the years. However, the lyrics of "Break the Cycle" focused on severing personal and generational bad habits to reach a place of love and understanding. The song *almost* got there, she admitted to *Time*. "The thing that I didn't get across is that I love my mom. We've been working on our relationship for a long time and we will continue to. That's the beauty of our relationship."

"You and Me"—the duo's eponymous track—was a bit more successful. The song's open-hearted lyrics express gratitude, and confess how much comfort and solace the other person brings. It came about after a conversation Green had had with his wife where he expressed how emotionally moving he'd found the experience of recording with Pink and the importance of their friendship to him.

Left: Pink and Dallas Green perform live onstage during the 63rd Annual BMI Pop Awards

rose ave. arrived at a time when duets were all the rage in the charts, led by the surprise hit standards album from Tony Bennett and Lady Gaga. It wasn't like either musician was hopping on a trend or striving for commercial gold. (In a nod to her status as the parent of a toddler, Pink noted lightly she was most familiar lately with the duets of Kermit the Frog and Big Bird hanging together on *Sesame Street*.) For Green and Pink, You+Me was a low-pressure way to take a break from the various stresses of their own careers, and create something unique that was just for them.

"This album is very personal for us," Green told *Time*. "I think one of the reasons we called it You+Me is because it was just an idea borne from the two of us being friends and wanting to sing together. When we were done we handed it to the label and said, 'Here, we did this. Do something with it.'"

They didn't have to put too much effort into convincing people to like it. *rose ave.* reached No. 1 in Green's native Canada and the US folk charts, and also landed in the Top Ten in Australia, Germany, the UK and the US, among other places.

Both Pink and Green have maintained their usual busy schedules since the release of *rose ave.* However, in a podcast that published in June 2021, Green revealed he had written "almost a whole new record" for You+Me. "We had been talking about trying to make another one of those, so I've been writing all these songs for that." Pink has also hinted in interviews, notably in a 2019 *Billboard* cover story, that she has some You+Me music brewing as well. It's clear that even if You+Me is dormant, the stories they've started aren't over; they're simply on pause, waiting for the right time for a new chapter to begin.

BEAUTIFUL TRAUMA

When Pink was a pre-teen, she saw Whitney Houston sing "The Star-Spangled Banner" at the Super Bowl. Houston's 1991 rendition was considered one of the greatest versions of the national anthem of all time; the vocalist exuded joy and patriotic pride while performing the notoriously difficult song. Pink was deeply inspired by Houston's appearance—and also vowed that she too would sing "The Star-Spangled Banner" one day.

Nearly two decades later, Pink finally received a chance to fulfill this wish, when she was invited to sing the national anthem at the 2018 Super Bowl. To make the experience even sweeter, her hometown team, the Philadelphia Eagles, was playing in the game. Unfortunately, as the day grew closer, Pink found herself sick with the flu, which she figured she caught from her kids. Still, she rallied to perform. Wearing a simple outfit—an off-white, satiny jacket over a ruffled shirt and wide-legged white pants—she approached the song with steely focus. In the end, although her voice was noticeably shakier and wavered a bit off-key in spots, she did an admirable job.

Despite being sick, some people didn't cut her a break. In fact, she found herself having to defend her performance after being criticized heavily for spitting out a throat lozenge before singing. On Twitter, she also clapped back at someone who said she "sucks" by responding, "Yeah, but at least I suck while singing our countries [*sic*] national anthem, and you just suck by yourself on a dirty couch. #winning." On the bright side, the Eagles also won the game, beating the New England Patriots 41–33, which took some of the sting away.

Prior to appearing at the Super Bowl, Pink had recently been exploring the ways life's ups and downs coexist. In October 2017, she released her seventh solo album, *Beautiful Trauma*, which arrived more than five years after her last solo album, *The Truth About Love*. Pink was hardly idle during this half-decade break, however. Among other things, she and Carey Hart welcomed a second child, son Jameson Moon.

Workaholic Pink didn't take too much time away from the studio. On the heels of recording her side project You+Me, she released the fizzy eighties pop throwback "Today's the Day" in September 2015. The relentlessly optimistic tune, which boasted lyrics about relishing the present moment, doubled as the new theme song to *The Ellen DeGeneres Show*; in fact, DeGeneres specifically commissioned Pink to create the song. To celebrate the release of "Today's the Day," Pink performed the song live in New York City on the TV show, with DeGeneres herself guesting onstage to dance and sing along. Pink later won a Daytime Emmy for the tune.

In 2016, Pink was recruited for another perfect-for-her project: recording music for the movie *Alice Through the Looking Glass*. The assignment led to a powerful cover of Jefferson Airplane's "White Rabbit" for the movie trailer. (Curiously, the song didn't end up on the soundtrack but did surface on a Japanese edition of *Beautiful Trauma*.) However, an in-your-face song called "Just Like Fire" did end up on the soundtrack. Co-written with Max Martin, Shellback, and Oscar Holter, the single is an empowered pop song with emo-rock and hip-hop undertones that encourages people to strive to reach their dreams.

The Dave Meyers-directed music video was a family affair, as the clip starred Pink, husband Carey Hart and

Previous: The *Beautiful Trauma* world tour opener at Talking Stick Resort Arena, Phoenix, Arizona, March 1, 2018

Opposite: February 4, 2018. Pink performs the "Star Spangled Banner" to open the Super Bowl at U.S. Bank Stadium in Minneapolis, Minnesota.

Left: Pink in the music video for "Just Like Fire," which featured in 2016's *Alice Through the Looking Glass*

daughter Willow. The latter chases a butterfly through a mirror that's a portal to a whimsical *Alice in Wonderland* world. In this fantasy land, Pink portrays multiple characters, including fiery chess pieces and tea-party visitor the Mad Hatter. Fittingly, she kept the *Alice in Wonderland* vibe going during a typically over-the-top May 2016 *Billboard* Music Awards performance. Not only did the performance *start* with her swinging over the crowd while hanging from a giant pocket-watch—it *ended* with her perched high above the stage on a clock hand, as the face is set aflame behind her. "Just Like Fire" peaked at No. 10 on the *Billboard* Hot 100 and reached No. 1 in Australia on the ARIA Charts, along with being nominated for a Grammy for Best Song Written for Visual Media.

Most poignantly, Pink, along with noted country songwriters and Nashville Songwriters Hall of Fame members Allen Shamblin and Tom Douglas, wrote a song, "Recovering," in honor of Céline Dion's late husband René Angélil. A heartfelt piano ballad, tailor-made for Dion's powerful voice, the lyrics speak to healing and reclaiming the self after a traumatic event. The Canadian superstar revealed to *Entertainment Weekly* that Pink reached out after Angélil's death specifically to offer her songwriting services. "She's a genuine person, and [it was] so generous of her to take the time to write a song for me during the most difficult time of mine."

Pink also couldn't say enough nice things about Dion. "She is like a magic lightbulb, walking around emanating light into the world," she told *Entertainment Weekly*. "When I wrote this song, there was such a simple need to it. I know everyone wants to hear Céline wail, I wanted to hear Céline's soul." Calling the Canadian icon "simply amazing," Pink added, "Getting

Opposite: Posing for photographers at the premiere of *Alice Through the Looking Glass*, El Capitan Theatre, Hollywood, US, May 23, 2016

to write a song for her is one of the biggest honors of my life."

The results blew Dion away, and, when the two women crossed paths at the 2016 *Billboard* Music Awards, she was grateful to be able to thank Pink in person. Dion told *Entertainment Tonight*, "I said, 'For you to take the time to really write a song, to give me a tool, a piece of luggage to help me to move forward to walk to keep going ... '"

In summer 2016, Pink checked another genre box off her career list: country music. She and country star Kenny Chesney had become acquainted in California, and he enlisted her to duet on the song "Setting the World on Fire." Laid-back and breezy, the tune details a romantic day with good tunes, inside jokes and a pleasant buzz. "Pink's voice holds so many feelings all at the same time: joy, desire, a bit of toughness, a little hurt," Chesney said at the time in a press release. "She's an incredible singer – and has this great tone that shines but has a little wear to it, but doesn't sound beat-up."

While outsiders may have scratched their head at the pairing, the collaboration made perfect sense. Both artists are down-to-earth, and their voices meshed perfectly, with Pink's smoky-but-tender delivery serving as a perfect foil to Chesney's warm approach. "To me, great singers are the ones who can get inside a song and capture the spark," he said. "When you hear Pink on this song, you believe her – and to me, that's everything the song required to come to life."

Chesney was thrilled with his Pink collaboration. In fact, he delayed the release of his new album, which ended up being called *Cosmic Hallelujah*, until October 2016 to make sure that the song could be included. His instincts were right: As it turned out, "Setting the World on Fire" wasn't just a pop hit—in the US, it peaked at No. 29 on the *Billboard* Hot 100—but it was a huge country hit, spending four weeks atop *Billboard*'s Hot Country Songs chart later that fall. For good measure, the song was also nominated for a Grammy, for Best Country Duo/Group Performance.

Pink's extracurricular activities continued into 2017. In March, she lent her vocals to the song "Waterfall," the debut single from the production duo Stargate that also included vocals from Sia. "Waterfall" reached the Top Ten of the US dance charts. That same month, she once again performed with childhood idol Billy Joel and his band at Dodger Stadium, joining them onstage for "Try." If Pink was nervous during the appearance, it didn't show; she was her usual vocal powerhouse.

These detours certainly helped Pink grow as an artist. However, few things informed the direction of *Beautiful Trauma* more than rest and quiet. In a conversation with *USA Today*, Pink noted that the half-decade between albums gave her more space to simply *be*. "Normally, since I was 19, I've gone, 'Make a record, promo, go on tour. Make a record, promo, go on tour,'" she said. "It's been this cycle. This is the first time I've been like, 'Take my daughter to preschool. Go on a date with my husband.' It's real life that's been on my mind."

Being able to do normal, everyday things changed her writing outlook, perhaps in unexpected ways. "I spent a year just writing slow, sad songs, thinking I was Adele," she told the *Los Angeles Times*.

However, by the time *Beautiful Trauma* was close to being finished, Pink had pivoted and expanded her vision. She wanted to have a better-produced album—and she was looking for a different kind of vibe. "There

DISNEY
ALICE

Previous: Pink's performance of "Just Like Fire" at the 2016 *Billboard* Music Awards in Las Vegas, literally lights up the stage.

Right: Performing live onstage during the 2017 MTV Video Music Awards, where Pink was honored with the Michael Jackson Video Vanguard Award

was no other goal than to not have an album full of slow, sad songs," she told *Entertainment Weekly*, in direct opposition to what she said in the previous interview. "It's always a reset in pop music. If you're taking a nap, you're having a 'comeback' the next time you put a song out. It's like starting over every time."

Beautiful Trauma was a sonic departure for Pink. Unlike the cameo-heavy *The Truth About Love*, the album puts her voice and perspective at the forefront; the only duet is "Revenge," a throwback hip-hop duet with Eminem. Accordingly, the album is audibly more cohesive, despite the fact Pink worked with co-writers both familiar (Billy Mann, Max Martin, Greg Kurstin, and Busbee) and new (including Julia Michaels and Jack Antonoff). And, as she noted with levity during an appearance on *Jimmy Kimmel Live*, she also swore *a lot* throughout the song's lyrics. "I went nuts," she said, noting she "didn't even realize" how many curse words were on it until she played the record in front of Willow.

"Since I was 19, I've gone, 'Make a record, promo, go on tour. Make a record, promo, go on tour.' This is the first time I've been like, 'Take my daughter to preschool. Go on a date with my husband.' It's real life that's been on my mind."

Profanity aside, *Beautiful Trauma* does have more mature music and themes, as Pink poured all the life experience she amassed in the previous five years into the project. In August 2017, she released the album's lead single, "What About Us." Co-written with Snow Patrol's Johnny McDaid and frequent Westlife collaborator Steve Mac, the song was a different kind of first single for Pink. Musically, the song resembles the light-on-its-feet pop favored by Coldplay, as it combines soft-glow piano with driving beats and keyboard-driven production. Thematically, the serious lyrics are focused on asking someone hard questions about their behavior—and the ways this person isn't showing up for support.

"Normally, I lead off with, 'What's your snarliest, loudest anthem for the first single?'" Pink told *USA Today*. However, that wasn't where her head was this time around, especially because she was now seven studio albums into her career. Instead of coming out with a brash, confrontational song, she followed the lead of her current mindset which was more introspective. "For right now, I've been more in a place of, 'What's right for me?' and 'Who am I?'; 'Marriage sucks' and 'marriage is rad,'" she told *USA Today*. "Long-term

relationships are hard work, and sometimes it gets really lonely."

McDaid confirmed to *Billboard* that the session was intense. "This is about [Pink] and it's about her opening up to saying something," he says, "and that's a really vulnerable thing to ask someone to do: To come in with two veritable strangers and to reveal your heart and to take whatever you create together in there and then to make that manifest in the world and everybody gets to hear it." Luckily, Pink was more than up to the challenge, he added. "She doesn't really inch forward, she leaps with kind of abandon into the fire and does it so beautifully that you have to go with her. It makes it feel really constructive and creative."

Opposite: Pink joins Axl Rose during Guns N' Roses' Not In This Lifetime...Tour, Madison Square Garden, New York City, October 11, 2017

Above: Performing onstage with Kelly Clarkson at the 2017 American Music Awards

"What About Us" isn't explicitly political—in fact, the song is written to be deliberately ambiguous—although in an interview with NPR (National Public Radio), Pink places "What About Us" in context with her family's long history with service, including her dad's military career and her mom's tenure as a nurse, and how her family always stood up for their beliefs. "I grew up listening to rock and roll and, you know, protest music," she said. "And I feel like with songs like 'What About Us' and 'Dear Mr President' and even 'Stupid Girls,' I'm doing my part a little bit. It's very clear who I am and what I believe in. I've been marching and protesting. And, yes, I could do so much more. Honestly, I could do so much more."

Pink achieved this with the "What About Us" music video, which did send a pointed political message. Directed by Georgia Hudson and featuring intricate moves choreographed by the Goldenboyz (a duo comprising RJ Durell and Nick Florez) the clip nods to protests against police brutality and the oppression of marginalized communities. "My absolute favorite thing in the world is dance, and it seemed the right way to talk about these ideas that the track presented, in an inclusive and exploratory way, which is also what the song demands," Hudson said in 2017. "I find that dance transcends semantics because it is driven by emotion and response—and that was what was necessary for the song."

Amid various backdrops—police cars with their lights, a helicopter spotlight, a late-night diner and a desert plain—Pink and a series of dancers embrace each other and move alone, writhing in ways that signal both anguish and catharsis. "We were on a trip with this video, and I think you can just see that," Hudson added. "The cast fed back such gratitude at having the chance to express their frustration and feeling towards the current political climate, that we could all feel for a moment the release of expression, of community." The song's message reverberated around the world: The single topped the charts in Australia and reached No. 13 in the US, along with being nominated for a Grammy for Best Pop Solo Performance.

In addition to "What About Us," *Beautiful Trauma* also featured another song about political and social advocacy, "Wild Hearts Can't Be Broken." The anthemic piano ballad was originally meant for the 2015 movie *Suffragette*, which covered the movement to secure women's right to vote. "You have to fight for what's rightly yours, which is rights and respect and love and kindness and compassion and you have to be willing to die for it," Pink told *Billboard*. "These women were." Accordingly, the lyrics are defiant and bold, and emphasize in no uncertain terms that the women are prepared to resist (and resist in drastic ways) to secure voting rights.

Those two songs illustrate *Beautiful Trauma*'s musical depth and Pink's evolution as a songwriter, though they're far from the only sophisticated moments. The

Left: Suspended 200 feet above ground, Pink performs "Beautiful Trauma" on the side of the J.W. Marriott hotel, as part of the 2017 American Music Awards

piano-dominated ballad "But We Lost It," co-written with Greg Kurstin, laments a painful breakup that occurs because a couple grew apart, while another Kurstin collaboration, the jaunty pop-rock anthem "Where We Go," is a song from the perspective of someone on the verge of starting over after a romantic split. "Barbies," meanwhile, is an acoustic, guitar-heavy song that longs for simpler, less complicated days when playing with dolls is the only thing on the calendar.

It's not easy to have so many songwriting collaborators and come up with such unique songs, but Pink told the *Los Angeles Times* that she's very particular about the music she works on with people like Max Martin and Jack Antonoff. "I have very honest conversations with them. If they play me something, I'm like, 'No, that could be anybody — I'm not doing that.' It has to be a little bit darker." Her *Beautiful Trauma* songs with Antonoff, rank among the record's best. Their partnership led to "Better Life," a sunshine-drenched R&B song, co-written with Sam Dew, about feeling insecure in a relationship, and the effervescent pop title track, which is about taking the good *and* the bad in life. "[Antonoff is] so lovable," Pink told *Entertainment Weekly*. "I thought we might have fun together, and I was right."

For all of *Beautiful Trauma*'s introspection, Pink did leave room for some fun. The gospel-influenced "I Am Here," which Pink wrote with her long-time creative foil Billy Mann, is an uplifting ode to surviving tough times. The music video for the album's title track was also lighter fare. Co-starring Channing Tatum as Pink's husband, the clip starts with the pair on a brightly colored, retro set straight out of the 1950s. Pink does stereotypical housewife things—cooking, cleaning, laundry, tending to the house—as Tatum spikes his coffee with booze and generally doesn't lift a finger to help. Later, however, after Pink downs a fistful of pills, the video shifts. The pair do a graceful dance number in the kitchen and then go on a journey of self-discovery. Pink finds Tatum in their closet trying on a dress, kicking off a sequence where she dons a suit and they do a gender-swapped, old-time dance; another sequence finds the couple dabbling in some light S&M fare.

In the end, that balance was important to Pink. "Life is fucking traumatic," she told *The Guardian* in October 2017. "There's natural disasters at every turn and there's kids starving and there's [then President Donald] Trump and there's all kinds of stuff going on, but there's beautiful people in the world that are having a blast and being good to each other and helping others." She added that her mood can skew "dark," so she strives to find balance. "I try to constantly remind myself that there's more good than bad."

Beautiful Trauma was another No. 1 smash around the world and would receive a Grammy nomination for Best Pop Vocal Album, although its release was just one high-profile musical highlight of her fall. A few weeks before the album hit stores, Pink received the Michael Jackson Video Vanguard Award at the 2017 MTV Video Music Awards. She performed an impressive medley of hits that mashed up eras and hits in unexpected ways. For example, Pink started the performance singing the lyric of "Get the Party Started" over the musical backing of "Raise Your Glass," while a later moment in her performance found her pairing elements of older song "Don't Let Me Get Me" over the somber piano of "Just Give Me a Reason." Appropriately, the performance

also referenced her music videos. During "So What," she hopped on a riding mower, which she rode on a catwalk off the stage as women held chainsaws aloft above her.

But it was her acceptance speech that stole the show. At the podium, Pink used the captive audience to share a story about a conversation she recently had with her daughter Willow while on the way to school. "She said, 'I'm the ugliest girl I know,'" Pink recalled. "And I said, 'Huh?' And she was like, 'Yeah, I look like a boy with long hair.'" After getting mad, Pink decided to put together a PowerPoint presentation full of "androgynous rockstars and artists that live their truth, are probably made fun of every day of their life and carry on, wave their flag and inspire the rest of us"—acts such as David Bowie, Freddie Mercury, Annie Lennox, Prince and George Michael, among others. Pink told Willow that she too is mocked for looking like a boy, "or I'm too masculine or I have too many opinions, my body is too strong," but then affirmed that she's not changing herself in response to mocking or hurtful comments. No hair changes, no body changes—nothing. "[I said] 'Do you see me changing the way I present myself to the world?'" Pink said. "[Willow replied] 'No, Mama.' 'Do you see me selling out arenas all over the world?' 'Yes, Mama.'" For good measure, Pink ended the

Below, left: January 28, 2018. Jenese Portee signs, as Pink sings "Wild Hearts Can't Be Broken" at the 60th Annual Grammy Awards, Madison Square Garden, New York City.

"Life is fucking traumatic. There's natural disasters at every turn and there's kids starving and there's Trump, but there's beautiful people in the world that are having a blast and being good to each other and helping others."

Left: Pink delights fans as she swings from a stage chandelier during her *Beautiful Trauma* world tour, 2018

speech with a powerful statement of unity and encouragement to be yourself in the face of cruelty: "We don't change. We take the gravel and the shell and we make a pearl. And we help other people to change so they can see more kinds of beauty."

The week of *Beautiful Trauma*'s release, Pink appeared on *Saturday Night Live*, where she performed "What About Us" and the album's title track. Days earlier, she had made a surprise appearance at Guns N' Roses' Madison Square Garden concert to perform the band's acoustic power ballad "Patience." Vocalist Axl Rose hinted that the performance was unrehearsed, although you wouldn't have known. Pink strutted onstage near the song's denouement, which features a soaring counter-melody, and nailed the high notes before coming back down to Earth and harmonizing perfectly with Rose.

A month later, Pink matched vocal pipes with another powerful singer, Kelly Clarkson. The women opened the 2017 American Music Awards with a stunning cover of R.E.M.'s "Everybody Hurts." Host Jamie Foxx introduced the song as a tribute to those who faced traumas in the previous year. "This year, more than perhaps any other in recent history, we needed the power of music to help us escape the news of the day," Foxx said. "We needed that power of music to help us heal from hurricanes, wildfires, hate, hatred-fueled violence: 2017 is the year that tested our faith." Fittingly, the pair's rendition of "Everybody Hurts" maintained the comforting lullaby vibe of the original, as their voices came together in soulful reverence.

During a normal awards show, this cover alone would have been enough to dominate headlines. However, later in the night, after darkness fell, she

Previous: Pink and dancers perform live onstage at Principality Stadium in Cardiff, Wales, during her *Beautiful Trauma* tour June 20, 2019

Left: Live onstage at Moda Center, Portland, Oregon, May 15, 2018

performed again. This time, Pink and crew set up outside of the theater—specifically, two hundred feet above the ground on the window-filled side of the J.W. Marriott hotel, Los Angeles—to perform "Beautiful Trauma." The performance wasn't for the faint of heart or anyone afraid of heights: Pink, sporting purple sparkly leggings, rappelled up the building side as if she was a pop music Spider-Man, performing gentle tumbles and acrobatic moves with another dancer who was also suspended in the air. The pair used the mirrored side of the building as their dancefloor, which was made to look flat with some camera sleight of hand. As the song progressed, several more dancers joined them to create a synchronized performance, windmilling their legs and using gravity (and the side of the building) to do spins. Pink somersaulted in the air multiple times, and backflipped and splayed out all her limbs, resembling a starfish.

In early 2018, she made waves on the Grammys with a performance of "Wild Hearts Can't Be Broken," although she kept her feet firmly on the ground while singing this time. This appearance nevertheless drew headlines because of its simplicity: Pink stood center-stage, sporting an off-the-shoulder white shirt tucked into plain blue jeans, while a sign language interpreter signed the song's lyrics next to her. The understated but inclusive presentation ensured nobody missed the song's important message.

Weeks later, Pink launched the *Beautiful Trauma World Tour* in Phoenix. Her set on this tour started

"The most important part of the show, no matter what, is if you can strip all the smoke and mirrors away and sound good live. But, shit, when you can have the smoke and mirrors I have, why not?"

off in a typically big way, with her swinging over the stage on a giant chandelier while singing "Get the Party Started." That wasn't the only time she went airborne: For "Secrets," she and a muscular dancer performed an incredibly intricate dance on ropes that at one point found her balancing in the air using only his feet and a hand for balance. That evolved into her spinning above the stage while squeezing her legs tightly onto one of the dancer's feet, with only light holding on his other leg for balance.

By now, it's almost easy to take Pink's aerial moves for granted, and she's well aware of how her moves draw attention and distinguish her shows from those done by other global superstars. "It makes it an experience as opposed to a musical concert," she told *Billboard* of all her live show stunts. "The most important part of the show, no matter what, is if you can strip all the smoke and mirrors away and sound good live. But, shit, when you can have the smoke and mirrors I have, why not?"

Pink's insight gets to the crux of why she's so good live: Even though she is one of the few performers able to pull off gravity-defying moves, she could also present a dynamic show without bells and whistles. That was certainly clear during the *Beautiful Trauma Tour*'s cover of choice, Nirvana's "Smells Like Teen Spirit." Wearing a grunge-like, plaid duster, she absolutely wailed on the electrified song, headbanging and jumping around like a rock star. In addition to this cover, the tour also featured a few special, one-off performances. In March, Dallas Green made a guest appearance at the Toronto show, and the pair performed a lovely, understated version of "You and Me." A few months later, Gwen Stefani made a surprise cameo in Los Angeles, she and Pink performing a spot-on, punked-up cover of No Doubt's "Just a Girl."

As the *Beautiful Trauma Tour* wound through North America into the summer and then to Australia and New Zealand for over two months starting in July 2018, Pink became stronger and stronger as a performer. However, the message within *Beautiful Trauma* only became clearer and more focused as the songs took on new life in concert.

"I think life is really traumatic, and it feels — even though it makes me sound like my parents to say this — like it's getting more so," she had told NPR in October of the previous year. "But I also think that there's really beautiful people in the world, and there's more good than bad, and there's love to be made and joy to be had." Pink then noted a quote favored by her dad—"I wish you enough"—and explained how that tied into her LP. "And what he means by that is, 'I wish you enough rain to be able to enjoy the sunshine. And I wish you enough hard times to be able to enjoy the easy bits.' And that's beautiful trauma to me."

In the years to come, Pink would experience plenty of pain and unexpected challenges along with moments of sheer beauty. Figuring out how to harness these extremes and find some semblance of balance would be one of her goals in the coming years.

Pink as a winemaker

Throughout her career, Pink has been an open book about everything in her personal and creative life, except for one thing: She secretly spent five years learning to become a winemaker. In fall 2018, she launched her own wine label, Two Wolves, named after a Cherokee parable.

"It has been a wonderful, five-year secret for me," she told the *Philadelphia Inquirer* after revealing her double life. "I haven't had a secret in a really long time, and it has been really fun getting a chance to learn a new craft on my own."

It's not unusual for musicians to launch their own wine label. However, Pink threw herself into the craft of winemaking with singular dedication. She signed up for online winemaking classes at Wine & Spirit Education Trust (WSET) and the University of California, Los Angeles (UCLA), squeezing in her studies while on tour. "I would jump off stage, sweating and shaking from adrenaline, and hurry to my computer to take my tests," she said on the Two Wolves website. To the *Philadelphia Inquirer,* she added, "I dropped out of high school to pursue my career in music, and it's the first time I felt like a student again—and I'm a really good student, it turns out." Pink also visited the world's greatest wine destinations—Bordeaux, Australia, South Africa, and California's own Napa and Paso Robles—and soaked up what knowledge she could from master winemakers.

However, nothing beats hands-on experience. In 2013, she and husband Carey Hart went all-in and purchased a multi-acre organic vineyard in Santa Barbara County, California. "After years and years of fantasizing and making terrible carboys of wine in my closets, we took our baby girl and left the city," she said, noting they upgraded and started making wine in their garage while continuing to hone their knowledge.

The immersive approach was transformative. "All of a sudden, when you start to love wine, I feel like it teaches you to pay attention to life," she told *Food & Wine* magazine. "It teaches you to pay attention to your food, where it comes from, what things smell like. Like, why did I never know the difference between a Granny Smith apple and a Red Delicious? Why have I never done a tomato tasting? Why do I not know how to describe the difference between a lemon and a lime?"

Of course, wine was an acquired taste for Pink, as it is for many people. Her initial exposure was via Manischewitz, a kosher wine served during the Jewish holiday Passover. (Pink's mom is Jewish, although the musician wasn't particularly religious growing up.) According to Pink, her mom's "terrible" taste when it came to wine, also informed her palate as she felt like drinking it was a "punishment." However, as she started touring and seeing more of the world, her manager opened her eyes to better possibilities.

The French wine Châteauneuf-du-Pape provided the gateway. "I fell in love," she said. "That was the 'aha!' wine for me, the first one. And then it sort of just became a rabbit hole." It wasn't just the taste that swayed her, however—she also loved the community around wine. "I learned that a great bottle of wine can be found anywhere, at any price," she stated on the Two Wolves website. "That sharing it with a stranger can turn them quickly to a friend and that this can be the catalyst to some of the best memories you will ever have to look back on."

"I prune vines while listening to Beck. I could do this—making wine—for the rest of my life. I mean, I'll probably be in a tutu in Vegas when I'm 69, but if I have to be in a tutu, at least I'll be drinking my own damn wine."

Perhaps unsurprisingly, Pink also values the community that's sprung up on Two Wolves. For starters, it's already a family affair—"Give her a hose and a cluster of grapes and she seems pretty happy," she says of daughter Willow's contributions—leaving open the possibility that someday both kids might end up running the vineyard. "I don't necessarily want my children to do what I do, and I know Carey doesn't want our children to do what he does," Pink mused. "But if I could give them custodianship of land and a love for it and something that they could really work hard at and feel proud of and do with me ... Who knows?"

Unfortunately for fans, Two Wolves isn't available in stores. Instead, the vineyard itself sells directly to people who sign up on the website to be members of the club. Previous vintages have included a grenache rosé described as a "warm, kind, big smile type of 'Hello'" that "makes you want to hug a complete stranger"; a graciano that's a "bright and zippy cherry bomb," akin to "cherry Pop Rocks or Cola"; and a syrah best paired with "dessert, coq au vin, mushroom pappardelle, or a rainy day."

Pink's love of wine and winemaking certainly doesn't take away from her music career—and it's also certainly no fly-by-night hobby. Visit the vineyard, and chances are you'll see Pink herself working outside, making sure that any upcoming harvest is the best it can be. "It's the hardest I've ever worked, physically," she told *Food & Wine*. "Way harder than a concert." She's certainly not complaining. "I prune vines while listening to Beck," she continues. "That's why I wanted to live here. I could do this—making wine—for the rest of my life. I mean, I'll probably be in a tutu in Vegas when I'm 69, but if I have to be in a tutu, at least I'll be drinking my own damn wine."

Above: Santa Barbara, California, where Pink and husband Carey Hart have a vineyard

HURTS 2B HUMAN

On February 5, 2019, Pink received a star on Hollywood Walk of Fame. With her husband, Carey Hart, and kids Willow and Jameson in tow, she called receiving the prestigious honor "surreal" and shared some empowering words about what the award meant. Noting her dad stressed to her the phrase "to thine own self be true," she then added: "There is a power in believing in yourself. You may not be the best that ever did it, you may not be the prettiest or the tallest or the funniest or the most talented—if you're stubborn and you don't give up and you work really hard — no one else can ever be you."

The same day she received the star, Pink dropped by *The Ellen DeGeneres Show* for an interview. She was a month away from launching more legs of her *Beautiful Trauma Tour*, a trek that was taking her back to North America and also to stadiums across Europe through the summer. During her appearance, however, she dropped a series of bombshells: In the coming weeks, she was filming a music video with the director of *The Greatest Showman*, Michael Gracey, and releasing a new single, "Walk Me Home." All of that was followed by the launch of a new album, *Hurts 2B Human*, in April.

"I usually go on tour and stop writing altogether but we just never stopped," she later told *Entertainment*

Previous: Performing live onstage during the 2019 Brit Awards, O2 Arena, London, UK, February 20, 2019

Above: Pink is honored with a star on the Hollywood Walk of Fame on February 5, 2019. Pictured is (L-R): Willow Hart, Jameson Hart, Pink, and Carey Hart.

"Opportunities kept coming up for me to work with all these incredible people, and I think that's what this record is all about: the village it took to create it."

Above: Musician Chris Stapleton joins Pink live onstage during her *Beautiful Trauma* tour, Madison Square Garden, New York City, May 21, 2019

Weekly. This quick creative turnaround was unusual for Pink. Not only was it unorthodox for her to release a new album so soon after her previous one—*Hurts 2B Human* emerged roughly eighteen months after *Beautiful Trauma*—but Pink had always closed out the touring and promotion cycle for a record before diving into the next one.

She had followed some of her own advice and decided to seize the day and strike while the creative irons were hot. Speaking to *USA Today*, Pink explained, she initially thought about releasing the EP, but realized that the project soon ballooned into something much bigger. "Opportunities kept coming up for me to work with all these incredible people, and I think that's what this record is all about: the village it took to create it." To say the album featured "incredible people" is an understatement. Alt-rock icon Beck, pop iconoclast Sia, country star Chris Stapleton, R&B upstart Khalid, and Imagine Dragons frontman Dan Reynolds were all on board, joining return collaborators such as Julia Michaels, Max Martin and Nate Ruess.

Right: Performing "Just Like Fire" at the 2019 Brit Awards, London, UK, where she was honored with the Outstanding Contribution to Music Award

Unsurprisingly, *Hurts 2B Human* is one of Pink's most diverse-sounding albums, with its nods to smoothed-out eighties pop-rock (the Beck and Greg Kurstin co-write "We Could Have It All"), scribbling electro (the Cash Cash-featuring "Can We Pretend") and avant-garde indie-pop ("90 Days," a collaboration with Wrabel that was heavy on processed vocal harmonies). However, *Hurts 2B Human* certainly has some thematic similarities with *Beautiful Trauma*, including trying to find silver linings in a world full of darkness and challenges. "I laugh more than anybody I know because I like to take the piss out of everything," she told *Entertainment Weekly*. "But I also have this contemplative, serious side and I know we're all a little bit anxious now. *Hurts 2B Human*'s songs are "a catalyst to all of us getting together to have group therapy and exorcise those demons," she added.

"Walk Me Home" certainly fits this bill. Co-written by Pink, Ruess and Scott Harris—the latter known for his work with Shawn Mendes—the song mirrors fun.'s layered pop and skyscraping choruses, along with sweet vulnerability: The protagonist asks for a companion to accompany them on a walk home, so they aren't alone with their thoughts. "Walk Me Home" was a Top Ten UK hit, and reached No. 1 on the adult contemporary charts in both Canada and the US.

On the day of the single's release, she appeared at the Brit Awards to accept the Outstanding Contribution to Music Award. As per usual, she kicked up her TV show performance a notch. Appearing wearing a cozy bathrobe and singing "Walk Me Home," she made her way to the stage through the backstage area, swapping her robe for a fluffy red jacket with a gigantic red train as she walked. Her walk ended with her hopping onto a perch that eventually lowered from the ceiling as she sang "Just Like Fire," accompanied by a display of massive pyrotechnics on the circular stage around her. That, in turn, led to a take on "Just Give Me a Reason" with a full choir and Bastille's Dan Smith taking the Nate Ruess parts. If that wasn't spectacular enough, she then performed "Try" in an indoor rainstorm, singing her heart out as water cascaded around her and a shirtless male dancer, as they both interacted with dazzling video projections. The appearance concluded with a powerful take on "What About Us" featuring pointed political messages on a video screen.

In contrast with the Brit Awards performance (and other Pink videos, for that matter) the "Walk Me Home" clip is almost low-key. Wearing a flowing, red dress, she strides, twirls and dances through empty city streets lit by neon signs and taxicab headlights. As she walks, the shadows of other invisible dancers appear alongside her, moving in their own graceful ways; at times, Pink is even swept off her feet into the air by unseen forces. The video's underlying message is that we're never alone on life's journey, even when we might feel like we are.

You might say that this message also explains Pink's eagerness to collaborate with so many different artists on *Hurts 2B Human*. However, some of these intriguing collaborations came together simply because she just asked if her dream duet partner was available. That was certainly the case with "Love Me Anyway," a song she co-wrote in Nashville with Allen Shamblin and Tom Douglas, the same team behind "Recovering," her song for Céline Dion. Country superstar Chris Stapleton was Pink's top pick for the song—and he said yes to a duet. That sparse ballad, "Love Me Anyway," echoes the theme of "Walk Me Home": The main character is drumming up the courage to make themselves vulnerable and ask if they're still worthy of love and support,

even if they're imperfect. Stapleton contributes raw, emotion-charged vocals in the background that function as an inner monologue, confessing things someone might be too scared to say out loud.

The title track, meanwhile, explores the dualities of life—even when you've found your person, that doesn't mean things are smooth sailing. Musically, it boasts a funky R&B vibe and vocals from Khalid, who offers sage words of wisdom. Khalid was her first choice to be on this song, and Pink admitted he agreed to appear because his mom's a fan of hers—a reason she took in her stride. "I've crossed over," she told *Entertainment Weekly*. "Someone I think is my age will walk up to me in an airport and be like, 'Hey! My mom loves you!' And I'm like, 'Fuck! I mean, thank you!'"

This song was particularly meaningful for her, as it represented her diving into and sitting with some painful feelings about the political and social upheavals going on in the world in 2019, particularly in the US. "It fucking hurts your heart," she admitted to *Entertainment Weekly*. "If you choose to remain open-hearted, then it's just going to hurt for a while." That's ultimately a good thing, she added, as realizing a shift is needed will encourage people to demand these much-needed changes.

As per usual, *Hurts 2B Human* also contains empowering songs about relationships and setting boundaries. "Hustle," the Dan Reynolds (with Jorgen Odegard) collaboration, is a swing-dancing, 1940s jump-jive on which she affirms that she doesn't suffer fools gladly, while the hip-hop-influenced Max Martin–Shellback

Above: Smiling after a powerful performance at the 2019 Brit Awards

Opposite top: Pink accepts the Outstanding Contribution to Music Award from Khalid at the 2019 Brit Awards

"I've crossed over. Someone I think is my age will walk up to me in an airport and be like, 'Hey! My mom loves you!' And I'm like, 'Fuck! I mean, thank you!'"

collab "(Hey Why) Miss You Sometime" grapples with that familiar feeling of longing for someone even though you know you're better off apart. "My Attic," meanwhile, asks someone to accept her who she is, even though she has all sorts of emotional baggage and clutter.

However, Pink stressed that *Hurts 2B Human* isn't as marriage-focused as some of her previous songs or albums. In a *USA Today* article, she mentioned one reason why: "Circle Game," a Joni Mitchell-referencing song about cherishing her father and still needing him even though she's an adult—but recognizing that their relationship has changed and is no longer as clear-cut as a parent–child dynamic. "I'm at that age where a lot of my friends are losing their parents and it's a really painful thing to go through," Pink said. "[The song] is about growing up and still feeling like that little girl, waiting for my dad to fix my problems and realizing that's not the way it is any more." Having kids shifted her perspective, she added: "I'm like, 'Wow, I'm your person.' There's a beautiful weight in that that just makes you reflect."

The song "Happy," meanwhile, is one of Pink's deepest and most probing songs. Lyrically, she lays it on the line about her personal insecurities, confessing dissatisfaction with her body, fears about the stability of her relationship and frustration at her inability to make changes for the better. She recognizes that her vulnerability and honesty is unique, but as she told *Entertainment Weekly*, "I don't feel like I'm any different than anybody else but maybe I'm just able to talk about it. I believe in therapy and I think music is therapy."

That Pink has always been so open about her mental health, and the challenges she's faced, sets her apart from other pop stars. It's a reflection of her humility, for starters, but also her willingness to be honest even when it's not necessarily flattering. "I believe in self-confrontation and just getting things out," Pink told *USA Today*. "What I love about therapy is that they'll

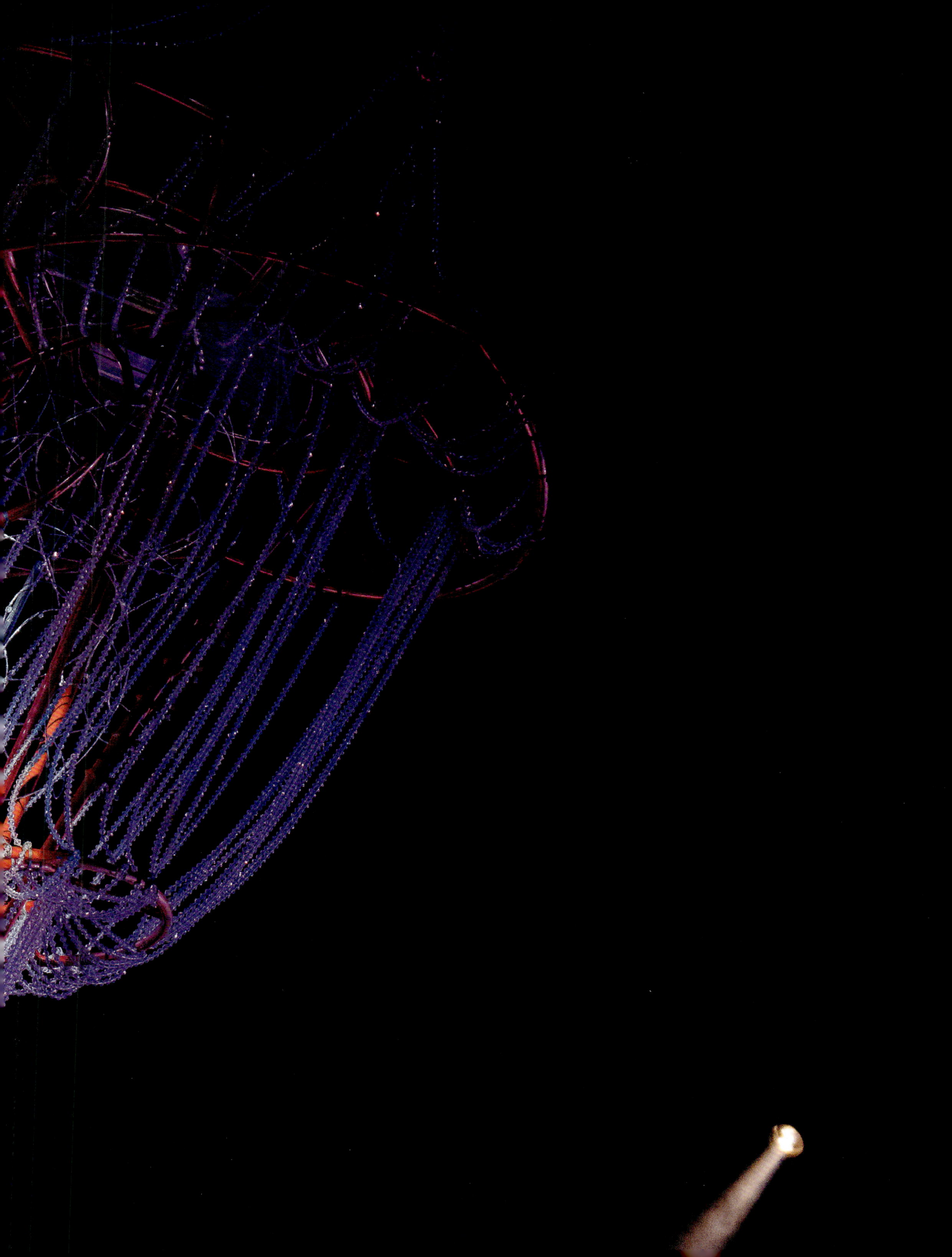

tell you what your blind spots are. Although that's uncomfortable and painful, it gives you something to work with." In a separate *USA Today* interview, she added, "I think the reason I can go to such uncomfortable places and be so honest is because I have a really healthy sense of humor ... I'm extremely self-deprecating." In other words, she tries to find the silver lining of even the darkest, most painful situations—and uses humor as a coping mechanism.

Released in April 2019, *Hurts 2B Human* reached No. 1 in the US—her third straight album to reach this peak—and also topped the charts in the UK, Australia, Canada, Ireland, Switzerland, and New Zealand. The successful release injected more energy into the ongoing *Beautiful Trauma Tour*; in fact, during the summer of 2019, she headlined stadiums throughout the UK and Europe, including two nights at Wembley Stadium that found her drawing an impressive 145,000 people overall. As part of this leg of the tour, she covered Bishop Briggs' "River," a perfect choice for her as the song is a cathartic, soul-blues rocker.

In August 2019, she finally finished the tour, which ended up featuring a staggering 157 dates and generated $397.3 million, according to *Billboard* Boxscore. That made it the second-highest grossing world tour ever by a solo female artist, eclipsed only by Madonna's Sticky & Sweet Tour. If that wasn't impressive enough, the *Beautiful Trauma Tour* (as measured by gross) was one of the biggest tours of all time, placing Pink firmly in the same league as heavyweight tourers such as The Rolling Stones, U2, and AC/DC. For good measure, she was also named Artist of the Year by *Pollstar*, a publication focused on the touring industry, as the *Beautiful Trauma Tour* ended up being the highest grossing global trek of 2019.

After the tour wrapped, Pink was in a contemplative mood when talking to *Billboard* about what

"I don't feel like I'm any different than anybody else but maybe I'm just able to talk about it. I believe in therapy and I think music is therapy."

her elaborate tours meant—and what she hoped to achieve. "We are going to be connected to ourselves and to each other," she said. "And we're going to connect to the fucking audience and the one person whose life is going to change tonight." Creating an inviting and welcoming atmosphere is also crucial, she continued. "Who's going to feel like they have a place in the world? Like they belong. Like diversity is OK. Like being your true self is OK. Like being fucking *loud* is OK. Like crying is OK. Like being not the best but feeling great is OK. It's all fucking OK. That's what we do. That's magic."

This ferocity is one major reason why Pink is such a dynamic force, although it's easy to see that maintaining this pace and intensity might be tiring. And so, to no one's surprise, Pink announced that she planned to take a well-deserved break in 2020 after her jam-packed last few years. This planned rest proved to be good timing because the Covid-19 pandemic ended up shutting down the music industry anyway from March 2020.

Unfortunately, that same month, during the early days of the pandemic when neither vaccines nor widespread testing were available, she and her three-year-old son, Jameson, caught coronavirus. They both became quite sick; in fact, Pink shared she had to use nebulizers to help her breathing because she has serious asthma.

She was even more worried about Jameson, who became sicker. "I've kept a journal of his symptoms for the past three weeks and mine as well," she said in a livestream. "He still, three weeks later, has a hundred [degree] temperature. It's been a different roller-coaster for both of us." Luckily, by early April the pair had recovered, although Pink was keenly aware of the challenges facing others who might not be so lucky with their health.

"It is an absolute travesty and failure of our government to not make testing more widely accessible," she wrote on Instagram. "This illness is serious and real. People need to know that the illness affects the young and old, healthy and unhealthy, rich and poor, and we must make testing free and more widely accessible to protect our children, our families, our friends and our communities." She donated half a million dollars to the coronavirus-focused Temple University Hospital Emergency Fund (her mom spent eighteen years working in the hospital's Cardiomyopathy and Heart Transplant Center) and the same amount to the City of Los Angeles Mayor's Emergency Covid-19 Crisis Fund.

Pink was hit with other health problems before the end of the year. In December, next to an Instagram photo of herself in the hospital, she noted 2020 was a "poop sandwich" and explained she had a staph infection and had just fractured her ankle. "Happy holidays everyone! Who wants a Negroni!"

Still, she found time to make some music when she wasn't feeling poorly. Most notably, Pink teamed up with Keith Urban virtually to record "One Too Many," a lighthearted, summery song about asking to be taken care of because you've had just a bit too much to drink. Urban told CMT (Country Music Television) that collaborating with Pink was always

Previous: Another show-stopping performance during day 6 of the Rock in Rio music festival, Cidade do Rock, Rio de Janeiro, Brazil, October 5, 2019

Opposite: Pink and Carey with their son, Jameson, at the Monster Energy Supercross VIP Event, Angel Stadium, Anaheim, California, January 18, 2020

"When she sings you can feel all of her humanity, her strength and her vulnerability and her courage and her fear and her swagger. All the colors of humanity . . . that's what sets her apart, she's truly extraordinary."

KEITH URBAN

on his wishlist, and when his co-executive producer Dan McCarroll sent him the track, he knew "One Too Many" was the perfect track for her. "Her voice is such an incredible gift," Urban said. "When she sings you can feel all of her humanity, her strength and her vulnerability and her courage and her fear and her swagger. All the colors of humanity she has in her voice when she sings that's what sets her apart, she's truly extraordinary."

The COVID-19 restrictions in place made collaborating in person challenging, although the pair rose to the occasion. Pink and Urban debuted the song on the ACM (Academy of Country Music) Awards in September 2020, with a performance that found them divided by a wall to protect their health. They also filmed a music video with each of them in a different location, on a premise suggested by director Dano Cerny. "He immediately sent back this idea of Pink being on an island and me being on a couch out in the middle of the ocean trying to get to her and I was in," Urban shared. "I just thought that was such a creative simple way to use this challenge and turn it into a strong storyline." The idea worked beautifully, as Urban (and occasionally some pals) live it up on comfy couches in the water beneath a brilliant sunset, as Pink sings her heart out on an idyllic beach.

In a case of turning tables, Pink's next major duet came with an artist she herself had long admired: the UK musician Rag'n'Bone Man, whom she initially had met in 2017. "By then I had already fallen in love with his voice, and when we met in person I quickly learned he has a beautiful soul, too," she said in a statement. "Since then, I knew I wanted to work with him one day." In April 2021, the pair released the hushed, soulful piano ballad, "Anywhere Away from Here," which he described as "an honest reflection of wanting to disappear from uncomfortable situations—about the vulnerabilities that we all face." As she did with Urban, Pink also appeared at a distance in the song's music video, which looked to be filmed in an old and once-grand theater now overrun by foliage and nature.

These two duets are extremely different but, as she told *Entertainment Weekly*, "I don't believe in genres. I just believe in music and speaking your heart." In 2021 and beyond, she would reveal sides of herself and her family never seen before—and start laying the groundwork for whatever her future was going to hold.

Right: Pink looms large via a projector screen as she sings "Anywhere Away From Here" with Rag'n'Bone Man, and the Lewisham and Greenwich NHS Trust Choir, to close out the 2021 Brit Awards

Pink and Parenting

It's no secret that Pink loves being a mom to her two kids with husband Carey Hart, Willow Sage and Jameson Moon Hart. "I made a choice a long time ago that I was going to have a successful family and that is my absolute No. 1 goal in life," Pink said on *Good Morning America*. While she's never shied away from including Willow and Jameson in all aspects of her musical career, she also makes it clear that nurturing family comes first. "I believe in affection," she told *People* in 2018. "I believe in needs being met and faith being implemented, and I believe in letting your kids know they can count on you, and that you'll be there."

Pink gave birth to Willow Sage on June 2, 2011. The name had sweet significance for the musician, she told *People*, starting with the fact she lived near a willow tree growing up. "It's the most flexible tree in nature and nothing can break it—no wind, no elements. It can bend and withstand

Opposite: Pink and Carey, with children Willow and Jameson, July 5, 2017, in New York City

Left: Pink holds the hand of daughter, Willow, backstage at the 2017 MTV Video Music Awards

anything. I love that sentiment. I want that for [my daughter]." Sage, meanwhile, is "cleansing and sacred," she added. "And it sounded great together. It doesn't hurt that her last name is Hart—flexible, cleansed heart."

Although Pink had intended to have a natural birth with Willow ("I was really looking forward to the whole rite of passage — giving birth perfectly present, unmedicated, in the way nature intended"), she ended up having a caesarean section after enduring two nights of labor. However, Pink bounced back quickly and, four months later, was already filming her role in the movie *Thanks for Sharing*, baby Willow in tow. "Everyone gives you this terrifying picture of no sleep at all, bickering which leads to divorce," Pink told *People*. "They made it sound like waterboarding. I think I've cried more than she has, and that's just because I'm emotional and a little nuts."

Still, that doesn't mean motherhood was easy. For example, in 2012, when Pink was due to perform at a music festival in Las Vegas, Willow fell and got a concussion, necessitating a trip to the hospital. "Somebody asked Carey how I've changed since I had Willow, and he said my claws have sharpened," she told *Glamour* in 2013. "They got longer too." In 2017, she and Willow got stuck in an elevator before a show. "Stuck in an elevator (it's getting hot in here) (love in an elevator) (livin in a box) #help," she wrote online, next to a photo of herself and Willow sitting on the floor of the elevator. Thankfully, they were rescued after not too long.

Pink is a dedicated mom who is determined to have a less turbulent relationship with Willow than she had with her own mother. "I had a strained relationship with my mom, which was both really, really beautiful and loving and really, really painful and empty," Pink told *Time* in 2014. "My greatest job in my life is to change that for my daughter. I would walk on fire to love Willow in a more wholesome way."

On December 26, 2016, Pink and Hart had their second child, son Jameson Moon. He also joined his mom on tour as soon as she hit the road again, touring to promote *Beautiful Trauma*. Although the work–life balance is difficult, Pink was up for the challenge of having two small children on tour. "I've never juggled so many damn plates in my life, but it's because I want to. I enjoy it," she told *Redbook*. "If I had nannies raising my kids and just wanted to be a rock star and party all the time, I wouldn't be successful and I wouldn't be happy." And while their upbringing is understandably different because of the time spent on tour— Pink noted her dressing room boasts a ball pit— both kids shy away from the trappings of stardom. In a *People* interview, she revealed Jameson wants to be an astronaut, while Willow attends gymnastics classes, reads Harry Potter books and has an active imagination: "She

"I've never juggled so many damn plates in my life, but it's because I want to. I enjoy it. If I had nannies raising my kids and just wanted to be a rock star and party all the time, I wouldn't be successful and I wouldn't be happy."

is convinced she's going to Hogwarts when she's 11, and I don't have the heart to tell her that she's not."

Pink's kids are so grounded because the family eschews the spotlight in favor of more low-key living. Off the road, the family lives in a more rural part of California. This locale has allowed the couple to raise both kids in an idyllic environment. "I've been a soccer mom for four years," she told *Entertainment Weekly* in 2017, doing normal-life things like bake sales and lemonade stands.

In a 2018 interview connected to her winning the title of *People*'s Most Beautiful Woman in the World award, Pink explained her parenting philosophy, clarifying that the family's house is rooted in acceptance on all fronts. "I feel like gender-neutral is in itself a label and I'm label-less," she says. "I don't like labels at all so I believe that a woman and a girl can do anything ... However, I have boys that flip dirt bikes and I have boyfriends that wear dresses. It's all okay to me. It's whatever floats your boat. So that's the kind of house that we live in." That doesn't mean Pink's house is a rules-free zone, however: "I always tell Willow, 'I'm going to teach you the rules so that you'll know how and when to break them.'"

Rebellion isn't necessarily in the cards just yet, however. Willow has followed in Pink's musical footsteps since infancy. When she was thirteen months old, she added bells to "How Come You're Not Here" and bass on "Timebomb," both of which appeared on *The Truth About Love*. The appearances came about organically, after Willow picked up the instruments in the studio. "[She] pulled out the bells and started banging on them, and I was like, 'Record it!'" Pink told *MTV News*. "And then she went up to the bass guitar on 'Timebomb' and started plucking away." For good measure, Pink noted lightly that Willow was already a better bassist than she was.

Willow's talent kept on evolving as she grew up. In October 2018, she and Pink recorded a cover of *The Greatest Showman* song "A Million Dreams" (and "A Million Dreams (Reprise)") for *The Greatest Showman Reimagined* soundtrack. Willow's voice was clear and confident on the rendition of the optimistic song, which imagines the dizzying possibilities available when you open your mind to dreaming.

And in February 2021, Pink released a song with Willow called "Cover Me in Sunshine." Self-recorded at home, the duet is a sweet folk-pop song with an insistent acoustic guitar riff. The pair harmonize together on the chorus, although Pink then lets Willow take the final verse by herself, so she has the last upbeat word. In an Instagram video, Pink noted "Cover Me in Sunshine" was uplifting. "It made us feel happy and so we're going to put it out for no other reason than that we hope that the song makes you feel happy. We thought we'd put it out around Valentine's Day as a big ol' hug and a kiss from us to all ya'll."

That unflagging support is indicative of Pink's parenting philosophy and the admirable way she can balance work and real life. "Touring with kids is impossible — and I did the impossible," she told *People* in 2021. "For a while there were a lot of other pop stars that were emailing me and calling me for the playbook on how to tour with kids, so I wrote a playbook for other moms. You just keep going. I'm just thinking about: 'Am I raising a kind person? What's it like to be my kid?'"

At the end of the day, however, she pushes these doubts aside and just revels in being a great parent and pop star.

Opposite: Jameson can't understand what all the fuss is about as mom, Pink, is honored with a star on the Hollywood Walk of Fame, Los Angeles, February 5, 2019

ALL I KNOW SO FAR

Like many people, Pink took her time re-emerging into the public eye after the Covid-19 lockdowns. In her case that meant she stayed off the road, hunkered down at home with family and only did the occasional music project. However, she appeared at the 2021 *Billboard* Music Awards with bells on after being named Icon of the Year at the event. Pink was in good company: Since the award was established in 2011, only nine other artists had ever won, including Prince, Stevie Wonder, Cher, Janet Jackson, Mariah Carey, Garth Brooks, Neil Diamond, Jennifer Lopez, and Celine Dion.

After a speech by childhood crush Jon Bon Jovi, who noted she had "a stage presence that only the greats have," Pink performed a set of greatest hits that showed off her rock'n'roll ferocity. In one of the night's sweetest moments, Pink's daughter Willow joined her to sing their duet "Cover Me In Sunshine," a track that they had recorded together at home and released in February 2021. The pair unfurled some rather impressive aerial moves on ropes, spinning around together both upright and upside down with the graceful form of ballerinas. Pink even let Willow spin around by herself at one point, a gesture that clearly meant a lot to the youngster. After her move, she hopped to the ground and embraced Pink, a touching hug that exuded both pride and happiness from both of them.

In March 2021, Pink released a documentary, *All I Know So Far*, via Amazon Prime. Directed by Michael Gracey, the deeply personal, eye-opening film follows her as she prepares to headline her two nights at Wembley Stadium in summer 2019. Not only does the film illuminate how incredibly hard she works to put on a live show, but it also draws back the curtain on what it's like raising kids and maintaining her marriage alongside a life on the road. Pink told *People*, "[Gracey] had never seen a mom changing diapers while having a creative meeting, and just the way that this big life intersects with being a normal, crazy family — there's something fascinating about that."

Speaking to *Forbes*, Gracey confirmed he received unprecedented access to Pink and her family, shooting footage until they fell asleep at night. That she "didn't separate her professional life and personal life" was certainly unique. "I found that a fascinating thing to capture. This is someone juggling being a mother and being a rock star, so I knew that there would be a comfort level that she would have in allowing me into what was a very personal and private life."

This kind of access made *All I Know So Far* much more interesting—and moving—than most tour documentaries. For starters, Pink isn't afraid to be gritty and honest about the ups and downs of parenting. At one point, she tries to stay mad at her youngest, Jameson, when he isn't listening, but he's being so goofy that she starts laughing instead. At another point, her daughter Willow gets very sick with a high fever and cough. Pink's concern over her health collides with the fear

Left and previous page: A beaming Willow joins mom, Pink, live onstage for a touching performance of their duet "Cover Me In Sunshine" at the 2021 *Billboard* Music Awards

she might get sick, which would put a wrench in her touring plans; the tension she feels taking care of her family *and* work life is palpable.

However, the documentary's details also make it stand out, such as times when Willow and Jameson are dancing around and playfully wrestling each other at show practice or the tender, playful moments when Pink and husband Carey Hart are shown taking care of the kids. It's also impressive to watch Pink direct her tour, whether it's showing what modifications need to be done to make the Wembley Stadium stage easier for her to navigate or critiquing her own performance by her own high standards. As a viewer, *All I Know So Far* is deeply inspirational, and makes you like Pink even more.

Along with the film, Pink released a new single, the cinematic "All I Know So Far," co-written with Oscar, Tony, and Golden Globe Award-winning songwriters Benj Pasek and Justin Paul, who are known for their work on the movie *La La Land* and the musical *Dear Evan Hansen*. "All I Know So Far" takes the form of Pink sharing wisdom with Willow, going over things she wishes she had known growing up—for example, that life has its ups and downs, and don't be afraid to get angry or speak your mind—and stressing that she'll always be there for support. Fittingly, this song too was nominated for a Grammy Award for Best Song Written for Visual Media.

For the video, she turned to her long-time collaborator Dave Meyers. "Since this song is sort of the story of my life and a letter to my daughter, making this video with Dave after we did our first video together 22 years ago is a really special, full-circle moment," Pink said of the clip. Reminiscing fondly about the "brother/sister relationship" he has with Pink, Meyers in turn said he was using the video to "capture the full breadth

Opposite: Singer Pink accepts the *Billboard* Icon Award from musician Jon Bon Jovi at the *Billboard* Music Awards, Microsoft Theater, Los Angeles, California, May 21, 2021

Below left: *P!NK: All I Know So Far,* US movie poster, 2021

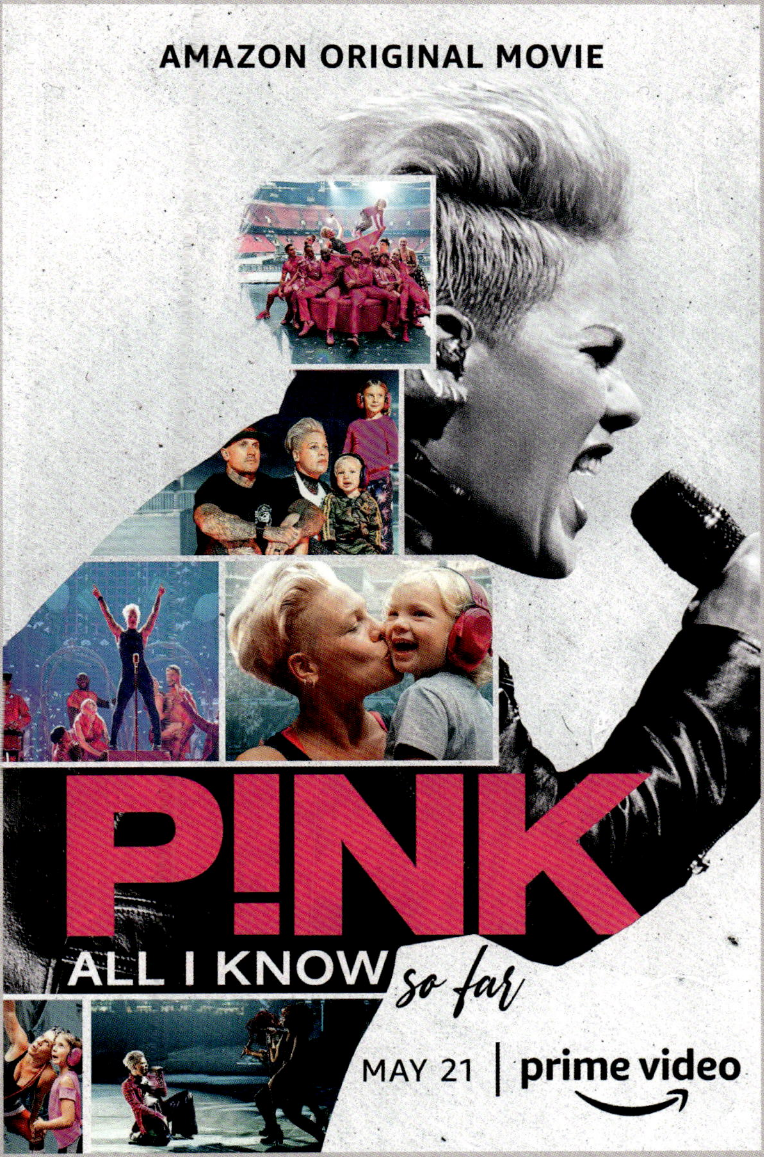

of who she is, where she has been and the troubled youth that's evolved into this idea of the power of community. It is where we are in the world right now and displays the idea that we really need each other."

The clip might be Pink's most ambitious yet, which is certainly saying something. Brimming with digital effects and bizarre scenes, it finds her navigating through a sci-fi, *Alice in Wonderland* reality where she encounters her real-life family and special guests, including Cher appearing as a sage deity and Judith Light portraying her mother. There are nods to her past—for example, she dresses like Rosie the Riveter as portrayed in the "Raise Your Glass" video and sails on a pirate ship with nods to the *M!issundaztood* album cover—and also references the song's supportive themes.

In the wake of the movie's release, Pink teased the possibility of new music, revealing to *ET Canada* in May 2021 that her next album would be "very honest," thanks to the turbulent last few years. "What an interesting time to be creative. What an interesting time to be thinking about the human experience and what we're all going through. I mean, it's different in every country right now, but yeah, man, it's been a wild ride the last year or so."

As per usual, however, her source material came from a familiar place. "Every time Carey pisses me off, I write a poem," she admits. "I've been making music since I was 16 professionally. So it's just been chapters," she says of her previous records. "If this whole thing will end up being a life story and an experience, each album is a chapter of that. So, yeah, it will be where I'm at now."

"Every time Carey pisses me off, I write a poem. If this whole thing will end up being a life story and an experience, each album is a chapter of that."

Unfortunately, 2021 brought even more tough real-life experiences to Pink's world. In August, her dad, Jim Moore, died of prostate cancer at the age of seventy-five. In response, she took to Instagram and shared two black-and-white photos of her dancing with her father: one taken when she was a kid, and one featuring her as an adult. "Til forever," she captioned the sweet tribute. A few months later, on what would have been her dad's seventy-sixth birthday, Pink posted a lengthier tribute on Instagram. "I don't even know that I can handle the cold hard truth that I miss you yet," she wrote, alongside a photo featuring a stack of donuts with a lit candle on top, placed carefully near his grave. "I wanna still act like this is one of those times that I'm busy and not calling. I can't feel this yet."

In 2022, Pink started revving up her public appearances once again, starting with a performance at a McDonald's corporate conference and an interview on

the final episode of *The Ellen DeGeneres Show*. Concert-wise, Pink also secured fall headlining slots at California's Ohana Festival and Austin City Limits Music Festival. However, in May, Pink officially presented her first full show after nearly three years away: a headlining set at the BottleRock festival in Napa, California. She dusted off some old favorite covers—4 Non Blondes' "What's Up?" as well as bluesy classic rock covers such as "Me and Bobby McGee," and "Babe, I'm Gonna Leave You"—in between knocking out hit after hit. Despite the outdoor setting, Pink figured out a way to go airborne. For the closing song, "So What," she changed up things and flew over the festival audience on wires like a zipline, allowing her to be nimble and do flips and twists in the air.

Opposite: Pink with her family during the making of documentary film, *P!NK: All I Know So Far* (2021)

Below: Pink with her children Jameson Moon Hart (left) and Willow Sage Hart (right), backstage at the 2021 *Billboard* Music Awards

Towards the end of her *Beautiful Trauma Tour*, Pink had keenly felt the dichotomy and demands of being both a hands-on mom and an international touring pop artist. "There have been many times when I have been sitting in the corner of arena bathrooms, crying and saying to myself, 'There's a reason why women don't do this, there's a reason why moms don't do this,' because it's fucking impossible at times," she had told *Billboard* in 2019. "The last couple of months, Willow was over it. She wants to be home and do BMX and swim team and gymnastics and all the shit that an 8-year-old wants to do. So she was asking to go home, and that's when I knew: From here on out, it changes."

Still, Pink can't resist the road. On October 6, 2022, she announced that she would be touring in the UK and Europe as part of her Summer Carnival Tour in 2023—including a whopping two headlining shows at London's BST Hyde Park—before returning to North America for further dates.

Following this announcement, the new music Pink had teased in 2021, off the back of her promotion for *All I Know So Far*, became a reality. *Trustfall*,

Left: Pink hugs her dad, Jim Moore, who died in 2021

Opposite: Pink performs on day 3 of BottleRock Napa Valley, California, May 29, 2022

Pink's ninth studio album was officially announced on November 18, 2022, on *Good Morning America*. With a release date of February 17, 2023, Pink stated that the album is "the best album she [I] had ever made" and explained how it had been inspired by many personal events in her life including the COVID-19 pandemic and her father's death. The album's lead single, "Never Gonna Not Dance Again," became available to stream on November 4, 2022, and she performed the song live for the first time at the American Music Awards on November 20, 2022.

Pink kept the remaining details firmly under wraps, and at the time of writing, there were no further details to share. However, the Summer Carnival Tour and *Trustfall* are yet further reminders of Pink's influence and impact on music. With the benefit of hindsight, you can see her imprint on modern music and the way pop and rock intersect. Back in the day, her teaming up with Linda Perry was unusual. Today, it's not uncommon for pop stars and rockers to collaborate. Travis Barker remains an in-demand drummer who's played live with rapper Machine Gun Kelly. Nuno Bettencourt from the hard rock band Extreme handled lead guitar duties for Rihanna for years. And even Lady Gaga collaborated with one of her heroes, Queen's Brian May.

Pink's commitment to following her muse in all sorts of different directions—even if these directions are unexpected or completely out of character—is also far more common today, in an era where the divisions between musical genres are porous. "I just needed to be who I was at that moment," she told *Variety* in 2019, of her musical philosophy. "I need to be who I am. I need to be authentic, and I've always been a kid who has been a lot of everything. I don't think that you should just have to be one thing."

Incredibly enough, Pink has never wavered from this philosophy, even as she's become more famous than she perhaps even dreamed. "If you listen to interviews, the things she said when she was 18 or 19 are the same things that she still says today," Gracey told *Forbes*. "She still cares about and values the same things. That's not normal. Forget about people in the public eye, we all evolve and have different thoughts and change our opinions and views, but she's always had such a strong sense of self."

This strength is a testament to how much Pink cares, both about her music and fans. In 2018, she stopped a concert in Brisbane, Australia, to hug and give comfort to a teenager named Leah who had lost her mom (also a Pink fan) a month before. "She told me that I looked pretty," Leah told a local newspaper. "She said, 'Oh, don't cry.' She said that everything was going to be okay. Then she signed my arm and we took a selfie. It meant everything. It was a dream come true."

Pink herself has experienced nearly all her dreams coming true. However, she's also never lost sight of all the women who came before her—and the ways in which they paved the way for her success. "I was the first in that sort of decade, but before that it's Blondie and Linda [Perry] and Madonna and so many other women," she told presenter Carson Daly in 2019. "Bette Midler was a trailblazer. I mean, there's Joan Jett. So I was just probably at that time a breath of fresh air because I was so rough around the edges and I wasn't tethered to the Earth at all."

Don't mistake that as Pink wallowing in nostalgia, however. She's not afraid of her past—but she's also more interested in personal growth, moving forward and seeing where life takes her in the future.

"There was a lot of great stuff going on then. There's a lot of great stuff going on now. So it's fun to still be a part of it," she said. "Every couple of years they're like, 'Oh this girl's gonna come in and take you out. You're gonna be done.' I'm like, 'First of all, that's not how it works. This is the music business. Everybody can win at the same time.' And good for her; that's great. That's wonderful. It's been an interesting journey."

CAN'T TAKE ME HOME (2000)

Track List (US standard edition):

1. Split Personality
2. Hell Wit Ya
3. Most Girls
4. There You Go
5. You Make Me Sick
6. Let Me Let You Know
7. Love Is Such A Crazy Thing
8. Private Show
9. Can't Take Me Home
10. Stop Falling
11. Do What U Do
12. Hiccup
13. Is It Love

Recorded: Boss Productions (Atlanta, GA); Brandon's Way Recording (Los Angeles, CA); Doppler Studios (Atlanta, GA); Patchwerk Recording Studios (Atlanta, GA); Purple Dragon Studios (Atlanta, GA); Record Plant (Los Angeles, CA); Soundtrack Studios (New York, NY); Triangle Sound Studios (Atlanta, GA); Unique Recording (New York, NY)

Released: April 4, 2000 (US)

Label: LaFace/Arista

Songwriting: Pink (tracks 1-2, 4, 9-10, 12-13); other songwriters include Terence Abney (track 1); Delouie Avant (tracks 12-13); Kenneth "Babyface" Edmonds (tracks 1, 3); Will Baker (track 10); Maurice "Big Reese" Sinclair (track 11); Jason Boyd (track 7); Kandi Burruss (tracks 2, 4); Neal Creque (track 6); Harold Frasier (tracks 9, 12-13); Darius Green (tracks 2); Sean Hall (track 6); James Hollins (track 11); Daron Jones (track 7); Kenneth Karlin (track 8); Michael Keith (track 7); Ezekiel Lewis (track 11); Andrea Martin (track 8); Ivan Matias (track 8); Lamont Maxwell (track 7); Obi Nwobosi (track 5); Quinnes Parker (track 7); Aaron Philips (track 13); Ainsworth Prasad (track 5); Kawan Prather (track 11); Steve "Rhythm" Clarke (tracks 9, 12-13); Marvin Scandrick (track 7); Kevin "She'kspere" Briggs (tracks 2, 4); Courtney Sills (track 7); Carsten "Soulshock" Schack (track 8); Marthony Tabb (track 5); Robin Thicke (track 6); Damon Thomas (track 3); Christopher "Tricky" Stewart (track 6); Pete Woodruff (track 10)

Production: Pink (track 13); other producers include Terence Abney (track 1); Kenneth "Babyface" Edmonds (tracks 1, 3, 5); Will Baker (track 10); Kandi Burruss (tracks 2, 4); Brainz Dimilo (track 5); Sean Hall (track 6); Daron Jones (track 7); Kenneth Karlin (track 8); Lamont Maxwell (track 7); P.A. (track 11); Anthony President (track 5); Steve "Rhythm" Clarke (tracks 9, 12-13); Kevin "She'kspere" Briggs (tracks 2, 4); Daryl Simmons (track 1); Carsten "Soulshock" Schack (track 8); The Specialists (tracks 9, 12); Christopher "Tricky" Stewart (track 6); Pete Woodruff (track 10)

Notable Personnel: Kevin "She'kspere" Briggs and Kandi Burruss, who co-wrote Pink's debut single, "There You Go," were also responsible for co-writing TLC's "No Scrubs" and Destiny's Child's "Bills, Bills, Bills."

Highest chart position on release: 10 (Australia), 12 (New Zealand), 13 (UK), 19 (Canada), 23 (Ireland), 26 (US), 85 (Germany)

Notes: A special edition of the UK version contains two bonus tracks, "Most Girls (X-Men Vocal Mix)" and "There You Go (Sovereign Mix)."

M!SSUNDAZTOOD (2001)

Track List (US standard edition):

1. M!ssundaztood
2. Don't Let Me Get Me
3. Just Like A Pill
4. Get The Party Started
5. Respect (featuring Scratch)
6. 18 Wheeler
7. Family Portrait
8. Misery (featuring Steven Tyler)
9. Dear Diary
10. Eventually
11. Lonely Girl (featuring Linda Perry)
12. Numb
13. Gone To California
14. My Vietnam

Recorded: DARP Studios (Atlanta, GA); Drive By Studios (North Hollywood, CA); The Enterprise (Burbank, CA); Larrabee Studios North (North Hollywood, CA); LP Studios (Sherman Oaks, CA); MF Studios (Monrovia, CA); Pinetree Studios (Miami Beach, FL); Sony Studios (Santa Monica, CA)

Released: November 20, 2001 (US); January 28, 2002 (UK)

Label: Arista

Songwriting: All songs co-written by Pink, except tracks 4, 8 and 11; other writers include Dallas Austin (tracks 2-3, 6, 12); Linda Perry (tracks 1, 4-5, 9-11, 13-14); Scott Storch (track 7) and Richie Supa (track 8)

Production: Dallas Austin (tracks 2-3, 6, 12); Damon Elliott (tracks 1, 5, 13-14); Marti Frederiksen (track 8); Linda Perry (tracks 1, 4-5, 9-11, 13-14); Richie Supa (track 8)

Notable Personnel: Pink fulfilled a career dream and dueted with Aerosmith frontman Steven Tyler on "Misery."

Highest chart position on release: 1 (Ireland); 2 (UK); 4 (New Zealand); 5 (Canada, Germany); 6 (US); 7 (Sweden); 14 (Australia); 17 (France); 24 (Italy)

Notes: Various versions of *M!ssundaztood* were released in different countries, including a European version with a different tracklisting and the bonus song "Catch-22."

TRY THIS (2003)

Track List (US standard edition):

1. Trouble
2. God Is A DJ
3. Last To Know
4. Tonight's The Night
5. Oh My God (featuring Peaches)
6. Catch Me While I'm Sleeping
7. Waiting For Love
8. Save My Life
9. Try Too Hard
10. Humble Neighborhoods
11. Walk Away
12. Unwind
13. Love Song
14. Hooker

Recorded: Battery Studios (New York, NY); Casa de P!nk (Sherman Oaks, CA); Crackertracks (Los Angeles, CA); Enterprise Studios (Burbank, CA); Mansfield Lodge (Hollywood, CA); Paramount Studios (Hollywood, CA); Skip Saylor Studios (Hollywood, CA); South Beach Studios (Miami Beach, FL); Steakhouse Studios (North Hollywood, CA); The Transplants' bus (various); Turtle Sound (New York, NY); Vibatorium (Los Angeles, CA); Westside Pacific (Malibu, CA)

Released: November 11, 2003 (US)

Label: Arista

Songwriting: All songs co-written by Pink; other writers include Tim Armstrong (tracks 1, 3-5, 8, 10-12, 14); Jonathan S. Davis (track 2); Damon Elliott (track 13); Brian MacLeod (track 7); Billy Mann (track 2); Paul III (track 7); Peaches (track 5); Linda Perry (tracks 6-7, 9); Eric Schermerhorn (track 7)

Production: Tim Armstrong (tracks 1, 3-5, 8, 10-12, 14); Jonathan S. Davis (track 2); Damon Elliott (track 13); John Fields (tracks 1, 6, 9-10); Billy Mann (track 2); Linda Perry (tracks 6-7, 9)

Notable Personnel: Future Oscar winner (and Trent Reznor collaborator) Atticus Ross contributed synthesizers and percussion; blink-182's Travis Barker contributed drums; Toto co-founder David Paich played organ; and Billy Idol guitarist Steve Stevens contributed riffs.

Highest chart position on release: 2 (Germany); 3 (UK); 8 (Australia, Canada, Ireland, Sweden); 9 (US); 12 (France); 24 (New Zealand); 51 (Italy)

Notes: The international version of *Try This* included the William Orbit mix of "Feel Good Time," which appeared in the 2003 film *Charlie's Angels: Full Throttle*, while the Japanese version has two extra songs "Delirium" and "Free."

I'M NOT DEAD (2006)

Track List (US standard edition):

1. Stupid Girls
2. Who Knew
3. Long Way To Happy
4. Nobody Knows
5. Dear Mr. President (featuring Indigo Girls)
6. I'm Not Dead
7. 'Cuz I Can
8. Leave Me Alone (I'm Lonely)
9. U + Ur Hand
10. Runaway
11. The One That Got Away
12. I Got Money Now
13. Conversations With My 13 Year Old Self
14. I Have Seen the Rain (featuring Jim Moore)

Recorded: Chateau Marmont (Los Angeles, CA); Conway Recording Studios (Hollywood, CA); Decibel Studios (Stockholm, Sweden); House of Blues Studio (West Hollywood, CA); The Magic Shop (New York, NY); MixStar Studios (Virginia Beach, VA); Phantom Studios (Los Angeles, CA); Pulse Studios (Los Angeles, CA); Remote Control (Santa Monica, CA); South Beach Studios, (Miami, FL); The Steakhouse (Los Angeles, CA); Tree Sound Studios (Norcross, GA); Turtle Sound Studios (New York, NY)

Released: April 4, 2006 (US)

Label: LaFace/Zomba

Songwriting: All songs co-written by Pink; other writers include Mike Elizondo (track 12); Lukasz Gottwald (tracks 2, 7, 9); Robin Lynch and Nikey Olovson (MachoPsycho) (track 1); Billy Mann (track 1, 4-6, 10-11, 13); Max Martin (tracks 2, 7, 9); Jim Moore (track 14); Butch Walker (tracks 3, 8); Rami Yacoub (track 9)

Production: Pink co-produced tracks 5 and 11; other producers include Josh Abraham (track 10); Al Clay (track 6); Mike Elizondo (track 12); Lukasz Gottwald (tracks 2, 7, 9); MachoPsycho (track 1); Billy Mann (track 1, 4-6, 10-11, 13); Max Martin (tracks 2, 7, 9); Butch Walker (tracks 3, 8)

Notable Personnel: The album's hidden track, "I Have Seen the Rain," is co-written by and features Jim Moore, Pink's dad.

Highest chart position on release: 1 (Australia, Germany, New Zealand), 2 (Canada), 3 (UK), 6 (US), 7 (France, Sweden), 9 (Ireland), 31 (Italy), 73 (Spain)

Notes: *I'm Not Dead* was the first album Pink released since departing from Arista Records, the label that had released her first few full-lengths. Accordingly, the record found her having a sonic awakening of sorts and recapturing the personal vibe and adventurous experiments of *M!ssundaztood*. *I'm Not Dead* was also the first Pink record to top the charts in Australia and New Zealand.

FUNHOUSE (2008)

Track List (US standard edition):

1. So What
2. Sober
3. I Don't Believe You
4. One Foot Wrong
5. Please Don't Leave Me
6. Bad Influence
7. Funhouse
8. Crystal Ball
9. Mean
10. It's All Your Fault
11. Ave Mary A
12. Glitter In The Air

Recorded: 3:20 Studios (Los Feliz, CA); Chalice Recording Studios (Los Angeles, CA); Chateau Marmont (West Hollywood, CA); Decibel Studios (Stockholm, Sweden); The Document Room (Malibu, CA); Electric Lady Studios (New York City, NY); Henson Recording Studios (Hollywood, CA); House of Blues Studio (Los Angeles, CA); The Magic Shop, (New York City, NY); Malibuddha Studios (Malibu, CA); Maratone Studios (Stockholm, Sweden); MixStar Studios (Virginia Beach, VA); Modern Dirt Laboratories (London, UK); Sha Recording (Malibu, CA); South Beach Studios (Miami, FL); Westside Pacific Studios (Los Angeles, CA)

Released: October 27, 2008 (UK); October 28, 2008 (US)

Label: LaFace/Zomba

Songwriting: All songs co-written by Pink; other writers include Marcella Araica (track 2); Nathaniel "Danja" Hills (track 2); Kara DioGuardi (track 2); Francis "Eg" White (track 4); Jimmy Harry (track 7); Tony Kanal (track 7); Robin Lynch and Nikey Olovson (MachoPsycho) (track 6); Billy Mann (tracks 6, 8, 11-12); Max Martin (tracks 1, 3, 5, 10); Shellback (tracks 1, 10); Butch Walker (tracks 6, 9); Pete Wallace (track 11)

Production: Al Clay (track 11); Danja (track 2); Eg White (track 4); Jimmy Harry (tracks 2, 7); Tony Kanal (tracks 2, 7); MachoPsycho (track 6); Billy Mann (tracks 6, 8, 11-12);

Max Martin (tracks 1, 3, 5, 10); Butch Walker (tracks 6, 9); Pete Wallace (track 11)

Notable Personnel: No Doubt bassist Tony Kanal contributed music, production and songwriting to several songs on *Funhouse*.

Highest chart position on release: 1 (Australia, Ireland, New Zealand, UK), 2 (Germany, US), 3 (Canada, Sweden), 4 (France), 5 (Czech Republic), 8 (Russia), 20 (Italy), 33 (Japan), 43 (Spain)

Notes: The international bonus track on the album is "This Is How It Goes Down," which features Gym Class Heroes frontman Travie McCoy. Like Pink's other albums, *Funhouse* was released in different versions in different countries across 2008 and into 2009. The album was also the first Pink record to top the UK charts.

THE TRUTH ABOUT LOVE (2012)

Track List (US standard edition):

1. Are We All We Are
2. Blow Me (One Last Kiss)
3. Try
4. Just Give Me A Reason (featuring Nate Ruess)
5. True Love (featuring Lily Allen)
6. How Come You're Not Here
7. Slut Like You
8. The Truth About Love
9. Beam Me Up
10. Walk Of Shame
11. Here Comes The Weekend (featuring Eminem)
12. Where Did The Beat Go?
13. The Great Escape

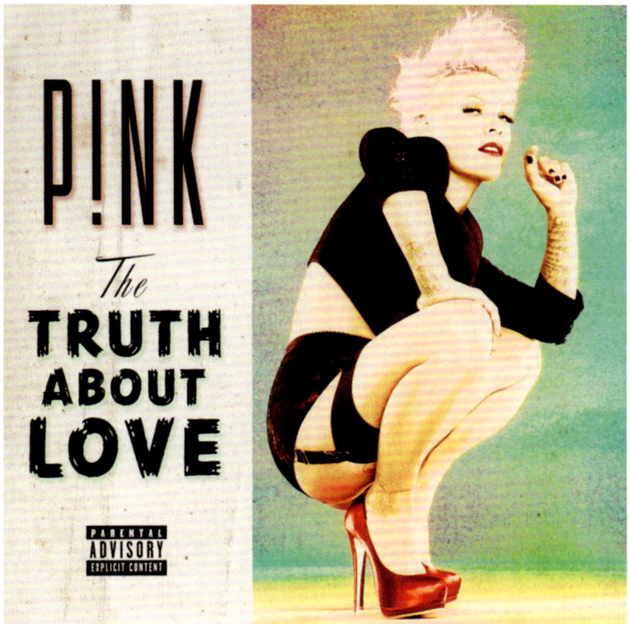

Recorded: The Ballroom Studio (Los Angeles, CA); Capitol Studios (Hollywood, CA); Conway (Los Angeles, CA); Earthstar Creation Center (Venice, CA); Effigy Studios (Ferndale, MI); Eldorado Recording Studios (Los Angeles, CA); Enormous Studios; Fishhead Music (Sweden); MixStar Studios (Virginia Beach, VA); The Modern Dirt Laboratories (London, UK); Ruby Red Studios (Santa Monica, CA); Super Sonic Scale (France); West Triad Studios (Venice, CA)

Released: September 17, 2012 (UK); September 18, 2012 (US)

Label: RCA Records

Songwriting: All songs co-written by Pink except track 3; other writers include Erik Alcock (track 11); Lily Allen (track 5); Jeff Bhasker (track 4); Busbee (track 3); Emile Haynie (track 1); John Hill (track 1); Pranam Injeti (track 11); Greg Kurstin (tracks 2, 5-6, 10); Billy Mann (tracks 8-9, 12); Max Martin (track 7); Marshall Mathers (track 11); Khalil Abdul Rahman (track 11); Liz Rodrigues (track 11); Nate Ruess (track 4); David Schuler (track 8); Shellback (track 7); Steve Daly and Jon Deep (Tracklacers) (track 12); Butch Walker (track 1); Ben West (track 3); Dan Wilson (track 13)

Production: Jeff Bhasker (track 4); John Brown (track 11); Emile Haynie (track 1); John Hill (track 1); Pranam Injeti (track 11); Greg Kurstin (tracks 2-3, 5-6, 10); Billy Mann (tracks 8-9, 12); Max Martin (track 7); Khalil Abdul Rahman (track 11); David Schuler (track 8); Shellback (track 7); Tracklacers (track 12); Butch Walker (track 1); Dan Wilson (track 13)

Notable Personnel: *The Truth About Love* boasted some big star power, including rapper Eminem, fun. vocalist Nate Ruess and UK pop star Lily Allen.

Highest chart position on release: 1 (Australia, Canada, Germany, New Zealand, Sweden, US), 2 (Ireland, UK), 4 (France, Italy), 5 (Czech Republic), 6 (Russia), 10 (Spain), 14 (Japan)

Notes: *The Truth About Love* was the first Pink record to top the charts in America.

YOU+ME, ROSE AVE. (2014)

Track List (US standard edition):

1. Capsized
2. From a Closet in Norway (Oslo Blues)
3. Gently
4. Love Gone Wrong
5. You and Me
6. Unbelieve
7. Second Guess
8. Break the Cycle
9. Open Door
10. No Ordinary Love

Recorded: Earthstar Creation Center (Venice, CA)

Released: October 14, 2014

Label: RCA Records/Dine Alone

Songwriting: All songs co-written by Pink and Dallas Green except track 10, which was co-written by Sade Adu and Stuart Matthewman

Production: All songs co-produced by Pink and Dallas Green

Notable Personnel: The album is a collaboration with Canadian musician Dallas Green, from the bands Alexisonfire and City and Colour.

Highest chart position on release: 1 (Canada), 2 (Australia), 4 (US), 6 (Germany), 10 (UK), 12 (Ireland), 37 (France), 50 (Italy)

Notes: The album contains a cover of "No Ordinary Love" by Sade, which was originally a hit in 1992. To date, it's the only album the pair have made together under the You+Me name.

BEAUTIFUL TRAUMA (2017)

Track List (US standard edition):

1. Beautiful Trauma
2. Revenge (featuring Eminem)
3. Whatever You Want
4. What About Us
5. But We Lost It
6. Barbies
7. Where We Go
8. For Now
9. Secrets
10. Better Life
11. I Am Here
12. Wild Hearts Can't Be Broken
13. You Get My Love

Recorded: Azteca Market (Glassell Park, CA); Bernie Grundman Mastering (Hollywood, CA); Earthstar Creation Center (Venice, CA); Eastside Studio (Nashville, TN); Landmark Studio (Nashville, TN); The Mastering Palace (New York, NY); MixStar Studios (Virginia Beach, VA); Willow-Valley (Göteborg, Sweden)

Released: October 13, 2017

Label: RCA Records

Songwriting: All songs co-written by Pink; other writers include Jack Antonoff (tracks 1, 10); Busbee (track 12); Sam Dew (track 10); Ross Golan (track 6); Oscar Holter (track 9); Jakob Jerlström (track 6); Tobias Jesso Jr. (track 13); Greg Kurstin (tracks 5, 7); Steve Mac (track 4); Billy Mann (track 11); Max Martin (tracks 2-3, 8-9); Marshall Mathers (track 2); Robin Fredriksson and Mattias Larsson (Mattman & Robin) (track 8); Johnny McDaid (track 4); Christian Medice (track 11); Julia Michaels (tracks 6, 8); Shellback (tracks 2-3, 9); Ludvig Söderberg (track 6)

Production: Pink co-produced track 13; other producers include Jack Antonoff (tracks 1, 10); Busbee (track 12); Ross Golan (track 6); Oscar Holter (track 9); Tobias Jesso Jr. (track 13); Greg Kurstin (tracks 5, 7); Steve Mac (track 4); Billy Mann (track 11); Max Martin (tracks 2-3, 9); Mattman & Robin (track 8); Christian Medice (track 11); Shellback (tracks 2-3, 9); The Struts (track 6)

Notable Personnel: Eminem once again makes an appearance on *Beautiful Trauma*, while glam rock band The Struts are credited with co-production and instruments on "Barbies."

Highest chart position on release: 1 (Australia, Canada, Czech Republic, Ireland, New Zealand, UK, US), 2 (France, Germany), 4 (Spain, Sweden), 5 (Italy), 28 (Japan)

Notes: The Japanese version of *Beautiful Trauma* features a cover of Jefferson Airplane's "White Rabbit."

HURTS 2B HUMAN (2019)

Track List (US standard edition):

1. Hustle
2. (Hey Why) Miss You Sometime
3. Walk Me Home
4. My Attic
5. 90 Days (featuring Wrabel)
6. Hurts 2B Human (featuring Khalid)
7. Can We Pretend (featuring Cash Cash)
8. Courage
9. Happy
10. We Could Have It All
11. Love Me Anyway (featuring Chris Stapleton)
12. Circle Game
13. The Last Song of Your Life

Recorded: Earthstar Creation Center (Venice, CA); Echo Studio (Los Angeles, CA); Grand Central South (London, UK); Henson Recording Studios (Los Angeles, CA); MXM (West Hollywood, CA); Record Plant (Los Angeles, CA); Roundhead Studios (Auckland, NZ); Studio Borgen (Partille, Sweden); The Village (Los Angeles, CA); Wolf Cousins Studios (Stockholm, Sweden)

Released: April 26, 2019 (US)

Label: RCA Records

Songwriting: All songs co-written by Pink except track 4; other songwriters include Samuel Frisch, Alex Makhlouf, and Jean Paul Makhlouf (Cash Cash) (track 7); Tom Douglas (track 11); Sia Furler (track 8); Teddy Geiger (tracks 6, 9); Beck Hansen (track 10); Scott Harris (tracks 3, 6); Anna-Catherine Hartley (track 6); Steph Jones (track 9); Ilsey Juber (track 4); Greg Kurstin (tracks 8, 10, 12); Billy Mann (track 13); Max Martin (track 2); Julia Michaels (track 4); Jorgen Odegard (track 1); Dan Reynolds (track 1); Khalid Robinson (track 6); Steve Robson (track 5); Nate Ruess (track 3); Allen Shamblin (track 11); Shellback (track 2); Ryan Tedder (track 7); Freddy Wexler (track 4); Wrabel (track 5); Alexander "Xplicit" Izquierdo (track 6); Alexandra Yatchenko (track 9)

Production: Pink co-produced tracks 11 and 13; other producers include Cash Cash (track 7); Simon Gooding (tracks 5, 11); Oscar Görres (track 9); Greg Kurstin (tracks 8, 10, 12); Billy Mann (track 13); Max Martin (track 2); Kyle Moorman (track 3); Jorgen Odegard (tracks 1, 6); Sal Oliveri (track 11); Dan Reynolds (track 1); Steve Robson (track 5); Shellback (track 2); The Struts (track 4); Ryan Tedder (track 7); Peter Thomas (track 3); Freddy Wexler (track 4); Wrabel (track 5)

Notable Personnel: *Hurts 2B Human* boasted a bevy of guest stars, including country star Chris Stapleton, R&B star Khalid, the electronic trio Cash Cash, and eclectic pop artist Wrabel. Co-writers on the album include Beck and Imagine Dragons' Dan Reynolds, while glam rock band The Struts once again co-produced a song.

Highest chart position on release: 1 (Australia, Canada, Ireland, New Zealand, UK, US), 2 (Germany), 4 (Czech Republic), 7 (France), 8 (Sweden), 14 (Spain), 27 (Japan), 28 (Italy)

Notes: *Hurts 2B Human* was the third Pink album in a row to debut at No. 1 on the *Billboard* Top 200 album charts.

ALL I KNOW SO FAR: SETLIST

(2021)

Track List (US standard edition):

1. Just Like A Pill
2. Who Knew
3. Funhouse/Just A Girl
4. River
5. Just Give Me A Reason (featuring Nate Ruess)
6. Time After Time
7. Walk Me Home
8. I Am Here
9. Fuckin' Perfect
10. MTV Video Vanguard Award Speech
11. Cash Cash Remix Intro/What About Us
12. Cover Me In Sunshine
13. All I Know So Far
14. Bohemian Rhapsody
15. We Are The Champions
16. So What

Recorded: All tracks recorded live at Wembley Stadium in June 2019, save for track 10 (recorded at MTV Video Music Awards in August 2017); track 12 (recorded at Pink's home); track 14 (live at the Sydney Entertainment Center, 2009); and track 15 (recorded at Rock in Rio 2019).

Released: May 21, 2021 (US)

Label: RCA Records

Songwriting: Pink co-wrote tracks 1-3, 5, 7-11, 13, 16; other co-writers include Amy Allen (track 12); Dallas Austin (track 1); Jeff Bhasker (track 5); Sarah McLaughlin (Bishop Briggs) (track 4); Thomas Dumont (track 3); Lukasz Gottwald (track 2); Scott Harris (track 7); Jimmy Harry (track 3); Robert Hyman (track 6); Mark Andress Jackson (track 4); Tony Kanal (track 3); Cyndi Lauper (track 6); Steve Mac (track 11); Billy Mann (track 8); Max Martin (tracks 2, 9, 16); Johnny McDaid (track 11); Christian Medice (track 8); Freddie Mercury (tracks 14-15); Maureen "Mozella" McDonald (track 12); Benj Pasek (track 13); Justin Paul (track 13); Nate Ruess (tracks 5, 7); Ian Scott (track 4); Shellback (tracks 9, 16); Gwen Stefani (track 3)

Production: Pink produced or co-produced tracks 1-9 and 14-16; other producers include A Strut (track 12); Jeff Bhasker (track 5); Greg Kurstin (track 13); Steve Mac (track 11)

Notable Personnel: Nate Ruess joined Pink at Wembley Stadium to perform "Just Give Me a Reason."

Highest chart position on release: 2 (Australia), 4 (New Zealand, UK), 5 (Germany), 8 (Canada), 13 (US), 14 (Ireland), 19 (Czech Republic, France), 67 (Japan), 100 (Spain)

Notes: Pink's second live album features covers of songs by No Doubt ("Just a Girl"), Bishop Briggs ("River"), Cyndi Lauper ("Time After Time"), and Queen ("Bohemian Rhapsody" and "We Are the Champions"), as well as Pink originals.

PICTURE CREDITS

T: Top; **B:** Bottom; **L:** Left; **R:** Right

ALAMY P8-9, P118, P167, P168-169, P173, P208 REUTERS/Mario Anzuoni **P12** REUTERS/Gary Hershorn **P23** Allstar Picture Library Ltd / Alamy Stock Photo **P24** © Paul Smith / Featureflash **P26** © RTCanova / MediaPunch **P29** Walik Goshorn/Media Punch/Alamy Live News **P30** ©Buena Vista/courtesy Everett Collection **P33** Jeffrey Mayer **P37** REUTERS / Alamy Stock Photo **P39** © Henry Mcgee/Globe Photos/ ZUMAPRESS.com **P46, P52** Fred Prouser REUTERS / Alamy Stock Photo **P62** Mary Ellen Matthews **P68** Chip East REUTERS / Alamy Stock Photo **P70, P72** ilpo musto / Alamy Stock Photo **P73** PA Images / Alamy Stock Photo **P109** Orban-Taamallah-Zabulon/ABACAPRESS.COM **P112-113** Peter Byrne PA Images / Alamy Stock Photo **P120-121** REUTERS/Gus Ruelas **P122** Tony DiMaio/ABACAPRESS.COM **P126** Brigette Supernova / Alamy Stock Photo **P136** Igor Vidyashev/ZUMAPRESS.com/Alamy Live News **P142-143** © Class 5 Films - Olympus Pictures **P151** Daniel DeSlover/ZUMA Wire/Alamy Live News **P156, P157B** Pictorial Press Ltd / Alamy Stock Photo **P162** Brian Kersey/UPI **P164-165** PictureLux / The Hollywood Archive / Alamy Stock Photo **P180-181** Katja Ogrin / PA Images / Alamy Stock Photo **P185** Gary Crabbe / Enlightened Images / Alamy Stock Photo **P193** WENN.com **P209** © Amazon Studios / Courtesy Everett Collection **P210** Andrew Macpherson/© 2021 Amazon / Amazon Studios / The Hollywood Archive **GETTY P2-3, P186, P192** Samir Hussein/WireImage **P10, P14, P38** Ron Galella, Ltd./Ron Galella Collection via Getty Images **P13, P204, P206** Kevin Mazur/Getty Images for dcp **P16** Todd Maisel/NY Daily News Archive via Getty Images **P17, P87** Jeffrey Mayer/WireImage **P19** Barry King/WireImage **P20-21** Paul Natkin/Getty Images **P21** Robin Platzer/Getty Images **P31** R. Diamond/ WireImage **P41, P74-75** Theo Wargo/WireImage **P44** Scott Harrison/ Liaison **P47** George De Sota/Liaison **P48, P65, P78-79** Steve Granitz/ WireImage **P49** PTEA/Getty Images **P50-51** Gareth Cattermole/Getty Images **P54** Ken Hively/Los Angeles Times via Getty Images **P56-57** M. Caulfield/WireImage **P58** Jim Spellman/WireImage **P59** WireImage **P61** Robin Platzer/Getty Images **P66-67** Kevin Kane/WireImage **P76** L. Cohen/WireImage **P81, P84** Dave Hogan/Getty Images **P82-83** ShowBizIreland/Getty Images **P85** GAB Archive/Redferns **P88, P102, P104, P114, P115, P116-117, P137, P139, P140, P212** KMazur/WireImage **P91** Jesse Grant/WireImage **P95** Kevin Kane/WireImage **P96** Chris Weeks/ WireImage **P97, P174-175** Kevin Winter/Getty Images **P98** Jo Hale/Getty Images **P106-107** Lester Cohen/WireImage **P123** Jean-Paul Aussenard/ WireImage **P124** Kevin Mazur/Getty Images for NARAS **P128** Bauer-Griffin/GC Images **P130** Mel Melcon/Los Angeles Times via Getty Images **P132** Jonathan Leibson/WireImage **P133** Kevork Djansezian/ AMA2012/Getty Images for AMA **P134-135** JazzArchivHamburg/ullstein bild via Getty Images **P144, P145** Kevork Djansezian/Getty Images **P146-147** Larry Busacca/Getty Images for SiriusXM **P152, P158-159** Chelsea Lauren/Getty Images for BMI **P157T** Paul Natkin/WireImage **P160, P172, P178-179** Kevin Mazur/Getty Images for Live Nation **P170-171** Christopher Polk/MTV1617/Getty Images for MTV **P182** Anthony Pidgeon/Redferns **P188** Alberto E. Rodriguez/Getty Images **P189** Zachary Mazur/WireImage **P194-195** Mauricio Santana/Getty Images **P196** Ari Perilstein/Getty Images for Feld Entertainment, Inc. **P198-199** JMEnternational/JMEnternational for BRIT Awards/Getty Images **P200** Robert Kamau/GC Images **P201** Matt Winkelmeyer/MTV1617/ Getty Images for MTV **P211** Rich Fury/Getty Images for dcp **P213** Steve Jennings/WireImage **REX SHUTTERSTOCK Cover, P7, P34, P42-43** Shutterstock **P20** Clive Dix/Shutterstock **P92** Mark Renders/EPA/ Shutterstock **P101** Georgios Kefalas/EPA/Shutterstock **P110** London Entertainment/Shutterstock **P148, P154-155** Casey Curry/Invision/AP/ Shutterstock **P176-177** Matt Sayles/Invision/AP/Shutterstock **P190-191** JM Enternational/Shutterstock **P203** Broadimage/Shutterstock

ALBUM COVERS P214 Darrick Warfield (art direction, design), Imagewerks Inc. (design), Daniela Federici (photography) **P215** Joe Mama-Nitzberg (creative direction), Jeff Schulz (art direction, design), Terry Richardson (photography) **P216** Jeri Heiden, Glen Nakasako (art direction, design), Andrew McPherson (photography) **P217** Glen Nakasako, Jeri Heiden (art direction, design), Andrew Macpherson, Deborah Anderson, John Heiden (photography) **P218, P219** Jeri Heiden, Nick Steinhardt (art direction, design), Andrew Macpherson, Deborah Anderson (photography) **P220** Jeri Heiden, Nick Steinhardt (art direction, design), Elliot Lee Hazel (photography) **P221** Jeri Heiden, Nick Steinhardt (art direction, design), Kurt Iswarienko, Ryan Aylsworth (photography), Sølve Sundsbø (interior photography) **P222** Jeri Heiden, Nick Steinhardt (art direction, design), Hueman (cover painting), Andrew Macpherson (photography) **P223** © RCA

SOURCES

Magazines and Newspapers *Cosmopolitan*, *Daily Mirror*, *Forbes*, *The Guardian*, *The Independent*, *The Intelligencer*, *The Irish Times*, *Los Angeles Times*, *New Musical Express*, *New York Post*, *People*, *The Philadelphia Inquirer*, *Rolling Stone*, *Time*, *Us Weekly*, *USA Today*, *Variety*, *Vulture*, *Women's Health*

TV and Websites www.alterthepress.com, www.archive.boston.com, BBC, www.billboard.com, www.britneyspy.com, www.cbsnews.com, www.digitalspy.com, www.dupreeperformingarts.com, www.ebmediapr.com, www.entertainment-focus.com, www.eonline.com, ET Canada, www.etonline.com, www.ew.com, www.genius.com, www.glamour.com, www.gulfnews.com, www.hollywood.com, www.instagram.com, www.jezebel.com, www.justjared.com, www.lostmediawiki.com, www.mamamia.com.au, www.mcall.com, www.mtv.com, www.music-promotions.co.uk, www.news.com, www.npr.org, www.onefinalserenade.com, www.pagesix.com, www.pajiba.com, www.pinkslibrary.wordpress.com, www.popcrush.com, www.redbookmag.com, www.rollingout.com, www.songwriteruniverse.com, www.tapeop.com, www.twitter.com, www.watchmojo.com, www.web.archive.org, www.web.rcarecords.com, www.en.wikipedia.org, www.yahoo.com, www.youtube.com